THE NEvv
COUNTRY COOK

A Twenty-First Century Look at British Cuisine

THE NEW COUNTRY COOK

A Twenty-First Century Look at British Cuisine

J. C. JEREMY HOBSON AND PHILIP WATTS

THE CROWOOD PRESS

First published in 2009 by
The Crowood Press Ltd
Ramsbury, Marlborough
Wiltshire SN8 2HR

www.crowood.com

British Library Cataloguing-in-Publication Data
A catalogue record for this book is available from the British
Library.

ISBN 978 1 84797 116 6

Typeset by Servis Filmsetting Ltd, Stockport, Cheshire

Printed and bound in India by Replika Press

Contents

Acknowledgements

This particular title is a result of a great deal of input, knowledge and help from so many kind and enthusiastic persons throughout the UK. Despite rigorous note-keeping, we are bound to have missed someone who offered invaluable information. To you we apologize whole-heartedly – it is due entirely to our inefficiency rather than the fact your expertise and guidance towards local contacts were inconsequential.

THE CHEFS AND RESTAURANT OWNERS
(In no particular order!)
Michelle Butterworth, Shelly's, Warrington, Cheshire; Steve Waters, Whitehall Hotel, Darwen, Blackburn, Lancashire; Robert Craggs, Cadeby Inn, Cadeby, Doncaster, South Yorkshire; Martin Wilks, Lords, Harrogate, North Yorkshire; Peter Simpson and Marcus Jefford, The Brasserie, Blenheim House, Etwall, Derbyshire; James Holah; Ernst Van Zyle, Stanneylands Hotel, Wilmslow, Cheshire; James Brown, The Ivy Brasserie, Grange Hotel, Clifton, York; Paul Widd at the Blackwell Ox Inn, York; Gerald Simpson, The Helpin Arms, West Yorkshire; Richard Hughes, The Lavender House, Brundall, Norfolk; Andrew and Jacquie Pern, The Star Inn, Harome, North Yorkshire (Andrew's recipes are taken from his own book *Black Pudding and Foie Gras*, which is available via *www.blackpuddingandfoiegras.co.uk* or by contacting The Star Inn directly on 01439 770397); Bryan and Susan Webb, Darley's Llandrillo, Denbighshire; Jayne O'Malley, The Town House, Solihull, Midlands; Simon Rogers and Dina Hanchett, The Boar's Nest, Kingston-upon-Hull, East Yorkshire; Martyn Nail, Claridges, London; Stephanie Moon, Clocktower Restaurant, Rudding Park, Harrogate, Yorkshire; Steve Stansfield, The Sun, Chipping, Forest of Bowland, Lancashire; Janet Hutchings, The Bell at Skenfrith, Monmouthshire; Vernon Blackmore, The Anchor Inn, Woodbridge, Suffolk; Andy Hook at Blackfriars Restaurant, Newcastle; all at the White Hart Hotel, Welwyn, Hertfordshire; Paul Yaxley, The Fox and Goose, Fressingfield, Diss, Norfolk; Uğur Vata, The Galley, Woodbridge, Ipswich, Suffolk; Mark Freeman, head chef at the Park Plaza Hotel, Cardiff; Martin Bland, owner of St Tudno Hotel and Restaurant, Llandudno, Conwy, Wales; Stephen and Norma Bond, Leicester's Restaurant at The Great House Hotel, Laleston, Bridgend, South Wales; Chris Birch.

We have particular reason to be grateful to Sarah Charles, and to Maria Taylor, Dominic Pattin and Andrew Evans at The Cottage in the Wood, Malvern Wells, Worcestershire. Also, to Sarah and Chris Whitehead and their head chef, Jonathan Waters, at Whites at the Clockhouse, Tenbury Wells, Worcestershire.

Thanks and acknowledgements must go to many others we have mentioned in the text, including: Dyllis Hatch; Sarah Rant; Alice Booth; Fiona Seddon; Tasmin Tate; Barry Phillips; Beryl Woodhouse; Carol Wilson; Beatrice Laval; Sally Olstead; Jenny Bristow; Sheila Benson; Sean Millar; Jane Robins; Rick Payne at Hall and Woodhouse; Brian Peterson; Terry Atkins; Carola Morrison; Fanny Watson, of The Organic Pantry, Newton Kyme, Tadcaster; Robinsons' Butchers, Chipping, Forest of Bowland, Lancashire; Broadfield Court Estate (Bodenham English Wines), Herefordshire.

And to those who made the whole thing possible: Francesca Hobson did a fantastic job of organizing our restaurant visits, whilst Rachel Kemmish very kindly made all the initial contacts. Thanks to all the staff at the Harrogate Tourist Board: to Adrienne Dyson; Dee Crowley; Claire Kendall; Edd Mcardle; Caroline at the Laguna Restaurant and Bar, The Park Plaza, Cardiff. Thanks too to The Language of Flowers, Tenbury Wells, Worcestershire; and to Natural Talents at Westlea Farm Shop, Alresford, Hampshire who very kindly gave us additional photographic opportunities. Hugh Johnson was generous in allowing us to use information found in *Hugh Johnson's Pocket Wine Book 2008* and thanks must also go to Philippa Talbott at Mitchell Beazley. Kate Harvey and Bloomsbury publishers granted permission to quote from *A Cook's Tour* by Anthony Bourdain.

Finally, some information has, as with the way of modern research, been gleaned from the internet. Many websites include that of others, and the information contained therein has, we hope, been passed through any copyright procedures. We have, as far as possible, obtained permission to include anything that is directly quotable, or recipes devised by a particular person. If we have omitted anyone, we can only apologize and request that those offended contact the publishers in order that amends may be made in any future reprints of this book.

Authors' Notes on Weights and Measures

Throughout the book, measurements are provided in both metric and imperial to ensure that the recipes are easy to follow. Since the conversions are not always exactly equivalent, the reader should use one or the other but not both. As an aid, it might be useful to include some general conversions from metric to imperial and also to the American cup system – to which the reader might find it useful to refer from time to time.

INGREDIENTS	METRIC	BRITISH MEASURE	AMERICAN CUP
Flour	115g	4oz	½ cup
Sugar	115g	4oz	½ cup
Butter	30g	1oz	2 tablespoons
Butter	225g	8oz	1 cup
Grated cheese	115g	4oz	1 cup
Breadcrumbs, fresh	75g	3oz	1 cup
Breadcrumbs, dried	60g	2oz	1 cup
Rice	225g	8oz	1 cup
Tomatoes, chopped	200g	7oz	1 cup
Apples	450g	1lb	3 medium size
Mushrooms, button	115g	4oz	1 cup
Honey/golden syrup	350g	12oz	1 cup
Mixed fruit	175g	6oz	1 cup
Nuts, chopped	150g	5oz	1 cup
Meat, chopped	450g	1lb	2 cups

Liquids	15ml	½fl oz	1 level tablespoon
	60ml	2fl oz	¼ cup
	125ml	4fl oz	½ cup
	175ml	6fl oz	¾ cup
	250ml	8fl oz	1 cup
	300ml	10fl oz/½pt	1 ¼ cups
	375ml	12fl oz	1 ½ cups
	500ml	16fl oz	2 cups
	600ml	20fl oz/1pt	2 ½ cups

NOTE: Exact liquid conversions are:
568ml/0.568L = 1 British pint (20fl oz)
473ml/0.473L = 1 US pint (16fl oz)

All recipes serve four unless otherwise stated.

Preparation and Getting Started

All of us have childhood memories of food: it may be the annual treat of fish and chips eaten out of their newspaper wrapping whilst on a family holiday at some seaside town; the way a favourite aunt indulged you with a 'special treat' whenever you went to visit, or even bad memories of the time you were made to stay in the school dining room when everyone else had got out to play – just because you hadn't eaten your rice pudding dessert. In the teenage years, recollections of food are like chronological reminders of important aspects of growing up and might include the sophisticated menu at the restaurant where you took your first 'proper' girlfriend in order to impress her, or the confusion encountered when you were taken out by your boyfriend and he ordered a dish that came accompanied by a bewildering array of eating implements – none of which you knew how to use. And then, in early adulthood, there were the exciting discoveries made on holidays both at home and abroad; dishes and menus unique to a particular country or part of the British Isles but which, when replicated at home, unfortunately never quite tasted the same as they did when you discovered them.

A restaurant manager of our acquaintance increased the number of table bookings – and his profits – almost overnight when, a decade or so ago, he tapped into people's food memories and began serving traditional foods rather than the complicated dishes in vogue at the time. At a time when it was generally thought that Lancashire hot-pot, steak and kidney pie, faggots, black pudding and other dishes generated from 'offal' were a poor man's food and that heart-attack inducing suet puddings had had their day, the popularity of this particular eating house proved that diners were seeking change.

The concept of eating traditional and locally sourced regional food is, in the twenty-first century, no longer alien to any of us – in fact, it is foremost in the minds of many when they go shopping and is the reason why farmers' markets do so well. 'Sustain' – an organization that supports the development and expansion of all aspects of the local food producing sector – desperate for an alliance of better food and better farming methods, have calculated that the ingredients of a typical roast dinner bought from a supermarket may well have travelled a total of 24,000 miles – whereas a similar meal bought from a farmers' market will have travelled no more than 80 miles.

There is considerable variety from region to region and county to county: some localities are inextricably linked with certain foods: Arbroath Smokies, Colchester oysters, Stilton cheese, Welsh Bara Brith and Derbyshire's Bakewell tart; and we had this in mind when we set out to find traditional and regional recipes that have been given a 'lift' and a 'twist' by imaginative chefs, restaurant managers, local producers and enthusiastic amateurs.

Traditional North Sea cod, given an imaginative lift by the addition of rocket leaves, sun-dried tomatoes, assorted olives and roasted red peppers (Uğur Vata, chef/patron at The Galley, Woodbridge, Suffolk, created this very visual dish by combining the best of British fish together with Mediterranean and eastern ingredients).

~ BASIC UNDERSTANDING ~

We were not disappointed in our travels. There are 'out there', many, many people who were prepared to talk to us; let us invade their kitchens and dining rooms and take away recipes for use within the pages of this book – their only reason for doing so being the fact that they wanted to share what they have discovered. Armed with many innovative ideas for modernizing a traditional recipe, we were, however, forced to rethink our original concept as a result of some of our conversations and we have been shown by numerous chefs that change for change's sake is not always a good thing. The old adage, 'if it ain't broke, don't fix it' sprang repeatedly to mind, especially when faced with comments from the likes of James Holah, who observed that food is 'sometimes refined so much that it's no longer what it started as. Some chefs' think "what can I do?" rather than think "should I do it?" Why ruin a perfectly good dish – ask yourself if you're improving or spoiling the original.'

Before rushing off to the kitchen, it therefore behoves the reader to truly understand some of the little nuances necessary for creating a successful meal using traditional and regional methods and recipes.

- Think about the food before you cook it: ask yourself 'do I understand what I'm doing?' and focus on whether things will work together. For example, dill with salmon or even something obscure such as Lancashire cheese with Eccles cakes!
- If using butter to cook with, don't use olive oil in the same recipe and vice versa: generally, butter should be used in hearty winter cooking and olive oil is best saved for Mediterranean-style recipes.
- If cooking for guests, tailor the menu towards them and where they come from in the country. Robert Craggs, who has been responsible for some of the best restaurants at home and abroad and is renowned for his innovative cooking, has discovered in his travels that 'you need different menus for north and south, and not just opposite ends of the country either – eaters in South Yorkshire will not eat what's on the menu in North Yorkshire. Portion control is different in various parts of the country and, traditionally, the northern diner is more likely to want to eat his dinner rather than waste time looking at it!'
- Focus on cooking recipes you like too: James Brown at the Ivy Brasserie believes that you should 'cook what you like to eat because you'll always cook better when you personally enjoy it.'
- Use local sources and seasonal products: Gordon Ramsay is famously quoted as saying, 'it should be a legal offence to use vegetables not in season'!
- It is possible to become confused as to a product's seasonality due to seeing it all-year-round in the supermarkets. To make the most of locally sourced vegetables and fruit, make an effort to learn what is in season and when.
- Good food, whether in the home or the restaurant, must begin with good produce – farmers' markets are excellent because it is possible to see the produce and talk about it with the stallholder who is often also the producer.

~ Eat Local ~

Of course, you cannot get more local than by producing food from your own back yard. Ideally, British food and cookery should develop from what is grown in the garden or reared on the smallholding where the interested amateur can grow a variety of foods for themselves. Unfortunately, this is not an option for many and so eating local equates to buying local and the purchase of produce sourced as close to home as possible should be high on everyone's agenda for several reasons, not least of which are the following facts:

- By exploring regional produce you will discover that there are varieties of vegetables with which you may yet be unfamiliar and meats from unusual breeds that add a new dimension to the recipe you are undertaking.

- Buying seasonal food is better for the environment and often cheaper; although as with any product, there is always a wide spectrum of prices.
- It also cuts down on polluting 'food miles' – the distance food has travelled from food to fork.
- Recently harvested food, and food which has travelled only short distances, is obviously fresher and will contain more nutrients – much better than fruit and vegetables that ripen on a plane.
- The willingness of the public to buy locally reared and grown meats and vegetables makes a difference to the way animals are kept in the pasture and whether good farming methods are used – there is undoubtedly more care taken in the production of quality regional produce.
- It boosts rural economy and ensures that farmers receive a fair price as well as raising our understanding of the countryside and traditional skills.

The British Isles is fortunate in that there are, despite the difficulties brought about by EU regulations, still small butchers who understand the traditional methods of producing tasty meat. The abundance of wild game and fish found locally is the ultimate free-range food: venison, for example, is fast becoming one of the most fashionable 'new' meats of the twenty-first century and other forms of game, including rabbit, pheasant and partridge, have surged in popularity in recent years. There are cheese makers supplying to local demand and growers ready and willing to sell to trade and private individuals via the extremely successful 'box schemes'.

Freshly harvested vegetables.

BOX SCHEMES

At The Organic Pantry, Tadcaster, Yorkshire, one of the biggest producers in the North of England, three generations of the Watson family are involved with the growing and production of over fifty varieties of vegetables, many of which feature in their particular box scheme. Basically, once signed up to the scheme, the customer is guaranteed to be supplied weekly or monthly with a selection of seasonal crops delivered to their own back door. Just how much variety is contained within the delivery depends on how much one is prepared to pay and the availability of crops at a particular time of year. For example, a large box of fruit, vegetables and salad (in season) may contain thirteen different varieties whereas a cheaper box of 'value' vegetables may only contain seven. It is, however, possible for the customer to choose individual vegetable varieties online from a selection of seasonal crops at the beginning of each week. Beware of some box schemes as, unlike the Watsons, who supply only organic produce grown on their own fields, some others are nothing more than a franchise and there is no real proof as to the origins of the fruit and vegetables sold.

In addition to vegetables, some operators of the box scheme will also supply their customers with meat, dairy and groceries delivered to your door. By doing so, they are turning the clocks back to the time when a local delivery from a local shop was the norm rather than the exception. With ever-escalating fuel prices, it is far more economical to have as much of your weekly shopping delivered as is possible – a van delivering on a carefully thought-out route will use less fuel than if you were to take the car in order to make a specific journey.

Many operators of the scheme also include recipes either online or as a weekly information sheet tucked into the delivery. In view of the rapidly increasing availability of less-than-common fruit and vegetables, this is undoubtedly a good idea as some customers have never come across certain types of vegetables before and a recipe explaining what to do with them saves a lot of head-scratching! Look out for boxes that include culinary herbs or even edible flowers, all of which add an interesting new dimension to regional and traditional recipes.

HEALTH AND ENVIRONMENTAL ISSUES

Organic crops, fruit and vegetables are produced without the use of unnecessary artificial pesticides or weed-killers: animal welfare is maintained without the routine use of antibiotics and vaccines, all of which benefit both health and the environment. Even organically processed food is different – hydrogenated fat and artificial colourings and sweeteners are banned along with other food additives that may be harmful to health. In addition, organic standards prohibit the use of genetically modified ingredients in food, as well as in animal feed. No wonder more and more people are turning to organically produced food because of health problems and allergies, and it's not just the customers: producers themselves are becoming more aware of health and environment issues and restaurateurs are beginning to look more and more towards locally sourced ingredients in an effort to cater for what their customers want. On a more general but no less important aspect, many local producers are considering the wildlife aspect of their enterprise and are entering into government-encouraged stewardship schemes or replanting hedges that were removed in the 'agribusiness' days of the 1980s.

Although local produce should not arrive covered in half the field in which it has been grown, remember that the pristine vegetables you may have become used to seeing have probably been factory-cleaned, unlike locally produced examples, which will probably be coated with a little dirt. This is in no way unhealthy: remember that mud is nature's preservative and that anything too clean is likely to have been damaged in the process. Sometimes, one shouldn't even peel a vegetable because the goodness is in the skin – get used to gently scrubbing the outsides or even arm yourself with a pair of rough-palmed gloves, which have been developed for such purposes and can be bought from many farm shops around the country.

Rough-palmed gloves will remove dirt without damaging the skin of vegetables.

~ WHAT MAKES A GOOD KITCHEN? ~

Not for nothing is the kitchen frequently referred to as being the heart of the home. Television shows and magazine articles frequently show kitchens to which we should, apparently, all aspire. Unfortunately, not all of us (in fact, hardly any of us) are proud owners of such products of the designer's art and even if we were, would they be more aesthetic than practical? We are led to believe that some new houses, especially those in the city developments, are being built with small kitchens containing not much more than a microwave because, if we can accept what we are told, most home owners in such a position take advantage of the close proximity of local restaurants in order to eat out for

The farm shop supplies fresh local produce and may operate a box scheme.

most of the time. Imagine the expense of such a lifestyle and, unless they are fortunate enough to eat in places such as we have found during our tour around Britain, imagine missing out on the opportunity to make wonderful meals from locally grown produce in your own kitchen – which certainly need not be as 'high-tech' as the designers would have us believe.

WHAT DOES A KITCHEN NEED?

It need not be large, but it should be carefully thought out. Perhaps the most important essential is plenty of work-space. No matter how much surface area there is, there is very rarely enough and most kitchens will, if space permits, benefit from the addition of a central table or island, which can be used for preparation or as a place to eat. Good lighting – both natural and artificial – is of utmost importance if you are cooking regularly and windows that open will be useful in letting out the steam and heat created by your activities!

Whether your oven should be electric or gas operated is down to personal choice. Of course, in keeping with the ethos of *The New Country Cook*, it should perhaps be a solid fuel Aga, Rayburn or something similar but, in reality, unless one is fortunate enough to have inherited such a beast when purchasing the house or you are refurbishing a kitchen completely, it will remain just a dream for many. There can be no doubt that an oven of this nature is a real treasure because of its different ovens and subsequent ability to cook at different temperatures. Likewise, the top hotplate can be used for either slow cooking or, set to a higher heat, the perfect medium for flash-frying and other preparation work. When it comes to standard ovens, perhaps the best combination is a fan-assisted electric oven (ideally with a spit-roast attachment), which ensures an even temperature at both top and bottom, together with gas-fuelled hob rings. Gas is great for instant heat and is very responsive: a pan of boiling milk, for example, will recede immediately once the gas is turned off, whereas the residual heat from an electric hob will mean that it will continue to boil – most probably all over the cooker's surface! One point to bear in mind is to ensure that the burners of a gas hob are always clean: lift out the moveable parts and brush them in soda water and, before putting them back, make sure that no hole is stopped up with residual grease.

Storage space is always at a premium, no matter how large the kitchen. With a little forethought, you can hide most of your equipment in cupboards and drawers, but it pays to plan where the items are most likely to be used before deciding where to keep things. Most cooks nowadays use a food processor or blender and, if you are intending to follow some of the bread recipes found in this book, a bread maker might not be a bad idea. Beware of buying (or allowing people to buy you) too many gimmicks and gadgets, which all take up valuable space and are very rarely used. Fill your space with a selection of assorted-sized pans, a steamer, a couple of heavy-bottomed casserole dishes (which can be placed on the hotplate as well as in the oven) and some decent frying pans. Always buy the best you can afford otherwise you will be forever screwing back handles that have become loose or, worse still, constantly buying new ones. Kitchen knives are another thing you should not stint on and, once again, buy the best you can reasonably afford – not normally ones to be impressed by brand names, we do however, on this occasion, think that a knife made by a well-known manufacturer is a 'must'.

Ladles and spoons, both slotted and solid, are essential kitchen tools.

KITCHEN INCIDENTALS

Cooking is not an exact science and your kitchen should not take on the appearance of a spotlessly clean laboratory: in fact, if anything, it ought to be more an artist's studio in which works of beauty are created! All jobs are, however, made easier with the right tools and bringing good quality food to the table is no exception. As well as the obvious pots and pans, you will, at some stage (and not long into your cooking), require two or three wooden spatulas (not metal, in case they damage the inner surfaces of your pans), which should be thin enough to lift the edges of pancakes and omelettes, as well as scraping out the mixings from a bowl. An assortment of mixing bowls, 'Pyrex' type for preference, will also prove essential, as will some ladles and spoons – both solid and slotted. Hang them on a rack if you like – at least that will clear valuable surface space, but in our opinion, there is nothing better than a utensil pot placed between the preparation area and the oven where everything you require will be instantly to hand.

Buy a colander that has secure handles – the cheapest often have ones that are riveted through soft metal and will pull out at the earliest opportunity. Although whisking and beating can be done with the aid of a kitchen fork, a whisk will, nevertheless, make the creation of sauces that much easier. Use a skimmer for removing surplus fat from a casserole or pot-roast and a funnel for returning unused oil back to the bottle. A roasting pan is handy, not only for the purpose in which it is intended, but also, when half-filled with water, will make an impromptu bain-marie. A vegetable peeler is easier to use than a knife, but better still, try to get away with gently scrubbing vegetables rather than peeling them, as to do so removes essential nutrients found in their skins.

Store vegetables carefully; a suitable rack placed in a dark but airy corner is possibly too important an item to be called an 'incidental' and it needs more consideration than one might otherwise suppose if you are not to be forever throwing away potatoes and carrots that have gone soft and soggy before you get the opportunity to use them. Much depends on their provenance: good quality local produce will undoubtedly last longer than that which has flown thousands of miles and been kept in cold storage in various stages of 'rest', but even so, a proper rack will pay dividends. Likewise, take care with your eggs: for some unknown reason, fridge manufacturers see fit to incorporate an egg tray in the door of some of their models and yet the fridge is possibly the worst place to keep them. Being porous, eggs will pick up and be tainted by other food products, such as cheese, that are kept in the fridge and they do not benefit from the cold temperature. Mind you, neither do they want keeping in close proximity to the oven where the spasmodic heat could make eggs heat up and cool down and, with such action, bring the risk of salmonella.

Finally, equip your kitchen with a plentiful supply of kitchen roll, tin foil, baking parchment, cling-film and freezer storage bags, all of which will be in frequent usage. It might also be a good idea to have a first-aid kit easily accessible in case of burns, scalds and minor cuts – include it and it will never be needed; forget it and, as sure as eggs are eggs (free-range or not!), it will be wanted straight away.

~ STORE-ROOM TIPS AND ESSENTIALS ~

Although the whole point of regional country cooking is to utilize local produce that is in season, there are, however, a few standard ingredients that should be in the cupboards and store-room of every cook. As with kitchen gadgets, it is, however, all too easy to become over-stocked with items bought on a whim and which, used once, get relegated to the back of the store-cupboard until thrown out years later when they are well past their 'use-by' date. Therefore, restrict yourself to the true essentials rather than being seduced by oils, for example, which come in attractively shaped bottles and contain a token sprig of herbs. It is far better to spend your money on ensuring the best quality of oil possible and rely on pretty-looking bottles being given as Christmas and birthday presents – which they surely will once your enthusiasm for cooking becomes known amongst friends and family.

FLOUR

Strong plain flour is normally used for bread-making and most recipes for cakes stipulate the use of self-raising unless you are making fatless sponges – in which case, use plain. Organic stone-ground plain flour is used by several chefs in their bread-making recipes, but in the average kitchen, too many varieties and types of flour are totally unnecessary and, once opened, bags of flour, especially brown, rapidly deteriorate, so it is as well to only keep as much as you intend to use over a fairly short space of time (one to three months). Keep it in the larder or, still in its bag, in a container made specifically for the purpose. Never mix old and new together when storing and always use up one batch before you open the next.

OILS

James Holah says never to mix butter and oil when cooking; it should be one or the other, but never both. Vegetable oil reaches a higher heat in the frying pan than does olive oil, which is why it is used in deep-fat fryers. Personally, I prefer to use good quality virgin olive oil for virtually everything (including a base for dressings and vinaigrettes), but others have, alongside their standard bottle of olive oil, one containing perhaps a ground-nut oil for frying and stir-frying, and the beautifully flavoured walnut and hazelnut oils for salad dressings. Jonathan Waters, head chef at Whites at the Clockhouse, sometimes flavours olive oil with herbs. Whatever you choose to do, always buy the best you can and store it in a dark place away from the heat of the hob.

VINEGAR

Balsamic vinegar is marvelous stuff! Again, as is the case with the various oils, buy the best you can afford, for there is a world of difference between the bog-standard supermarket brands and the really top quality varieties. Balsamic vinegar adds a touch of sweetness to many dishes and is perfect for salad dressings – as are the alcohol-based vinegars such as sherry and cider. Red or white vinegars are used in several recipes in this book, but it is possible to use herb and vegetable vinegars to flavour salads, cold meats, casseroles or grills. Traditional malt vinegars have their place in the kitchen of *The New Country Cook* and can be used in piquant sauces, marinating, and for soused foods like herrings and mackerel. Pickling vinegars can be bought 'in season' and do away with the need to add vinegars *and* spices to your recipe, but if you are making your own pickles and chutneys from scratch (and, after reading the section beginning on page 184, there is no reason why you shouldn't), use simple plain vinegar. Whatever type is thought necessary; always store it in a dark place to prevent a loss of colour.

MUSTARDS

A tin of good old-fashioned Colman's mustard powder is a useful stand-by in any kitchen, but it is possible to use whole seeds in pickles and, should you be of a mind, soused herrings. Grainy French mustards are great added to casseroles or pot-roasts and can, of course, be spooned straight from the pot and to the side of the plate in order to add 'zest' to a huge variety of dishes – although, in our opinion, any guest or household member who liberally dollops mustard onto their food without first of all tasting it should, like those who do the same with salt, be taken out and shot!

SALT AND PEPPER

Beware the person at the dinner table who demands salt before even putting a forkful of your carefully prepared food to their mouth! It is, to our mind, an insult to your culinary skills if the delicate nuances and flavours already included in the recipe, are polluted by an additional taste. However, *during* cooking, the addition of both salt and pepper is, in most cases, warranted. Every chef to whom we've spoken mentioned Maldon sea salt as their first priority, closely followed by table and cooking salt.

As for pepper, well, it seems there is only one kind as far as most are concerned and that is the aromatic black peppercorn, which is technically, a spice, but we are not going to stretch a point here! Keep the peppercorns whole and grind them as needed by the use of a wooden peppermill. Whole white (and indeed, pink) peppercorns are available, but seem to be rarely used by the professionals.

SPICES AND DRIED HERBS

Cinnamon, both in its ground form and sticks; vanilla pods; dried chillies; whole coriander, ground cumin; curry powder; all-spice and sachets of mixed spices and herbs are all essential in the kitchen store cupboard. So too, are the seeds of coriander, fennel, cumin and caraway, and of course, nutmeg and cloves.

Although there can be nothing better than freshly chopped herbs that will give a special flavour not found in the dried varieties, there is still very much a case to be argued for the use of dried herbs, but it is important not to be too heavy-handed in their use because the initial drying of them seems to concentrate their flavour potential and they could overpower the taste of some of the more subtle dishes, especially fish. Dry your own by hanging them in bunches or laying them out on a tray in the sunshine (in the absence of sunshine, dry them in an oven that has recently been used for cooking and is therefore warm but switched off). After a couple of days in the sun, leave them at room temperature for two weeks, but turn them regularly until they are crisp and flaky. The leaves can then be crushed and stored in airtight containers until required. Use them to good effect in casseroles and stews.

Perhaps we should have included a pestle and mortar in amongst the kitchen incidentals, as they are handy to have around when dealing with spices and herbs and take up little space. Jamie Oliver suggests that the heavy, stone types are better than the smaller, more delicate ones – and he should know!

SAUCES
A bottle of tomato ketchup would, perhaps, be considered an insult to the chef if it were to be used on a prepared dish when brought to the table, but it has many uses during the actual preparation of some recipes. Even a pan of minced beef being used for nothing more elaborate than an ingredient of shepherd's pie can benefit by being flavoured by a good squirt or two of tomato ketchup and it is of frequent use in the Hobson household when, during tasting, a potentially bland recipe is in need of a little more 'bite'. Add it to a multitude of dishes and you will be surprised how often the subtle taste is commented on but rarely identified! Try also mushroom ketchup as an alternative in the same dishes. Lea & Perrins Worcestershire Sauce gives, according to the makers, 'that instant richness to meat dishes' and, during the course of our tour around Britain, it is surprising just how much it is relied upon by professional chefs and amateur cooks alike. It is also a very valuable ingredient in the creating of marinades. Soy and oyster sauces also have their devoted followers.

Some store-room essentials are invaluable in preparing marinades.

TINS AND JARS

No-one can call their store cupboard a store cupboard without it containing at least one tin of whole, peeled plum tomatoes! Sun-dried tomatoes bought preserved in oil are a very interesting addition to salads and starters – indeed spread over a freshly made bruschetta, they are the best snack ever. Beans and lentils have their uses, but some, such as white haricot beans, tend to loose some of their distinctive flavour during cooking and, for this reason, the dried varieties are often a better option. Nevertheless, it will pay to keep some tins of both.

Red chillies, bought pickled in vinegar, are an exceptionally useful adjunct to the store cupboard: yes, you can manage without them, but once they become a part of your cooking armoury, it is surprising just how often you'll find yourself using them – treat them with care; avoid wiping your eyes or cuts having handled them and make sure that the digestion of any guests is not likely to be upset by their inclusion.

Although it need not be bought expressly for inclusion in the store cupboard, as it will most likely be in the kitchen anyway, another useful item is orange marmalade. Again, like tomato ketchup, a small amount will sweeten a dish and give it a tangy flavour. Add a little to gravy, especially when it is being used as an accompaniment to meats such as duck.

PASTA AND RICE

Keep a stock of dried pasta and rice, as they provide an accompaniment to many of the recipes in this book. Spaghetti and tagliatelle are both good standbys, but so too are linguine, penne and farfalle. As for rice; a packet or two of long-grain pilaf or basmati covers most eventualities, but for the risottos you will need either Arborio or Carnaroli. The chefs who have been kind enough to offer risotto recipes have generally stipulated their personal preferences, which can be seen on the appropriate pages.

SUGAR

Granulated, caster, soft-brown and muscovado sugar are all mentioned in this book, particularly in the sections dealing with puddings and cakes and biscuits. Sugar in its various forms is also used for most, if not all, of the chutneys and pickles, and so the storing of several types might just disprove the dictate of not allowing your store cupboard to become too cluttered with unnecessary items. *Farmhouse Cookery – Recipes from the Country Kitchen* (Reader's Digest, 1980) mentions the interesting fact that, weight for weight, all refined sugars are equally sweet, but that the faster it dissolves, the sweeter it seems. Granulated sugar is the most popular and widely used sugar, as well as being the cheapest. Caster sugar dissolves even more quickly than granulated and, as well as therefore imparting more sweetness to the recipe in which it is being used, it gives a smoother texture. The various types of brown sugar used in the various recipes throughout this book, range in colour from fawn to dark brown and their inclusion will have a subsequent effect on the colouring of whatever is being produced. Keep all sugars out of even the slightest damp.

The Starter

Why have starters? Perhaps it would be more correct to call them appetizers, for that is exactly what they should be – a colourful and interesting taste of things to come, rather than a meal in itself. A starter need not be very complicated or elaborate, but it ought to have something of a 'wow' factor about it; it is surprising just how an ordinary arrangement of simple, fresh ingredients can be 'lifted' by the addition of a garnish of light green herbs or a slice of orange or lemon. If your main course is complex, make your starter the opposite – if it is hot and spicy, make your starter cool and plain.

For some unknown reason, many cooks panic at the idea of producing a starter, why this should be we've no idea, as all it takes is a little imagination to come up with something totally unique. They need not be expensive either; a few thin strips of smoked fried bacon laid appetizingly over a carefully arranged salad and served with a home-made dressing costs next to nothing, as would a smattering of herb-infused cream cheese spread onto a thin slice of ham, which is then rolled into a type of roulade.

Many of the starters listed here would, with perhaps an increase in quantities, make the perfect supper dish. However, if they are to be used as intended, it is important not to over-face your guests with great heaps piled onto their plate – in this instance 'small, but perfectly formed' is definitely the way to go!

~ FISH ~

Fish is generally classified by three generic groups: 'white' fish (where the oil is only found in the liver of the fish) such as cod, haddock and sole; 'oily' fish (where the oil is present in all parts of the fish), which is thought by many nutritionists to be the healthiest and includes salmon, trout, mackerel and herring; and 'shellfish', which are themselves divided into two further sections: crustaceans (lobster, crab, crayfish and prawn), and molluscs (oysters and mussels). Whilst white and oily fish are normally available all the year round, shellfish should only be purchased in season and, in keeping with the ethos of this book, from as local a source as is possible.

Only buy from an experienced, interested and enthusiastic retailer. They are not there just to sell you fish: they should also be able to advise on the best variety for the particular dish you have in mind and must have the knowledge to be able to remove the intestines and swim bladder; cut a salmon steak as you like it and otherwise prepare what you have chosen in readiness for the pan or oven.

Cullen Skink

No doubt someone, somewhere, will be able to say how this Scottish soup got its name – the authors however, remain in ignorance!

350g/12oz smoked haddock
600ml/1pt milk
600ml/1pt fish stock
1 onion, finely diced
450g/1lb mashed potatoes
25g/1oz butter
15g/½oz fresh parsley, finely chopped
salt and pepper

Put the haddock, milk, stock and onion in a saucepan, bring slowly to the boil and simmer for 5 minutes. Remove the fish and leave to cool. Strain the liquid into a clean saucepan. Remove the skin and bones from the smoked haddock and break up the flesh with a fork before returning the fish to the liquid and stirring in the potatoes and butter. Heat gently, stir in the parsley, season to taste and serve immediately.

Confit of Salmon with Roast Scallop, Pickled Fennel and Goat's Cheese Fondant

Martin Bland, owner of St Tudno Hotel and Restaurant, Llandudno, Conwy, Wales, serves modern British cooking with 'classic sauces and intense flavours'. The chefs endeavour to offer a wide variety of food sourced locally including Welsh lamb, lobster, crab and sea bass.

For the confit of salmon with roast scallop
4 × 75g/3oz cubes salmon
600ml/1pt goose or duck fat
4 scallops
pea shoots to garnish
knob of butter
salt and pepper

Bring the fat up to 150°C (300°F) in a saucepan, place the salmon in the pan so it is completely submerged, leave on stove for 5 minutes. Remove and allow to rest for a further 15 minutes. Heat up a frying pan (ensuring it is very hot), place scallops in and cook for approx 45 seconds, each side. At the last 20 seconds, add a small knob of butter, season and set aside.

Salmon fish cake with samphire as prepared at the Fox and Goose, Fressingfield, Diss, Norfolk.

For the pickled fennel
2 bulbs fennel (shredded)
600ml/1pt pink grapefruit juice
115g/4oz sugar
1 star anise
pinch cayenne
pinch salt
8 strands saffron

Place all the ingredients into a thick-based pan, with the exception of the shredded fennel, bring to a rapid boil and continue until caramelized. At this point add the fennel, simmer on a low heat until the texture of marmalade has been achieved before chilling the mixture in the refrigerator.

For the goat's cheese fondant
115g/4oz soft goat's cheese
60ml/2fl oz double cream
½ teaspoon Wasabi

Place all the ingredients into a blender and blend until smooth, correct the seasoning and chill.

To assemble the whole, place the salmon confit in the middle of the plate, work the fennel pickle around the salmon, quenelle the fondant and place on top of the salmon, along with the roast scallop, garnish with pea shoots and serve.

Fried Mackerel with New Potato Salad and Beetroot Chutney

We have included this quick and simple recipe from Vernon Blackmore of The Anchor, Woodbridge, Suffolk, in amongst the fish starters, but it would just as equally make a lovely light lunch or summer's evening supper dish.

For the mackerel with new potato salad
4 mackerel fillets
500g/1lb new potatoes
125g/4½oz green beans (blanched)
4 tablespoons your favourite vinaigrette
flour and seasoning
olive oil

Fried Mackerel with New Potato Salad and Beetroot Chutney.

For the beetroot chutney
1 large beetroot, finely diced
1 medium onion, finely diced
4 tomatoes, roughly chopped
250ml/8fl oz malt vinegar
sugar to taste

Firstly, prepare the beetroot chutney by placing the tomatoes and onion in a pan with the vinegar and bring to the boil. Reduce to a medium heat and simmer until it starts to thicken (approximately 15–20 minutes). Add in the beetroot and simmer for a further 15 minutes. Sweeten according to taste. Take off the heat and leave to one side. This can be prepared a day ahead and keeps up to a month in the fridge.

Next, boil the potatoes, drain and mix with the blanched green beans. Dust the mackerel skin with lightly seasoned flour and place skin side down in a non-stick pan on a medium heat. Lightly season the flesh, turn over when the skin has crisped up (check by lifting one edge), cook for 1–2 minutes then remove from the heat.

Mix the potatoes and the vegetables with the vinaigrette, lightly season and divide onto the four plates. Place the mackerel fillet on top and drizzle with olive oil. Add a spoonful of chutney to the side of the vegetables.

Pan Seared Scallops with Laver Bread and Cockle Cake, and a Light Lemon Froth

Leicester's Restaurant at the Great House Hotel, Laleston, Bridgend, South Wales, also prides itself on using organic local produce, including fresh fish caught in nearby Porthcawl.

Serves two
3 king scallops (coral off)
50g/2oz laver bread (Welsh seaweed)
20g/¾oz cockles washed (not in vinegar)
2 shallots diced
1 lemon, zested and juiced
50ml/2fl oz cream
50g/2oz butter
olive oil
glug of white wine
salt and pepper
1 egg

Place the seaweed and cockles along with half the shallots in a mixing bowl. Mix together with one egg and shape into six mini round pates.

For the sauce, sauté off the remainder of the shallots in the butter, then add the lemon zest and juice, then reduce until sticky. Then add a splash of wine and finish with the cream using a hand blender. Froth up the sauce. Season to taste.

Cook the scallops in a non-stick pan with a little oil and season each side for 2½ minutes. Leave to rest.

Whitby Crab and Prawn Cocktail.

Whitby Crab and Prawn Cocktail

Leading northern chef, Robert Craggs, Chef Director of the Cadeby Inn, Doncaster, South Yorkshire, can be regularly seen carrying out live cookery demonstrations at Food and Restaurant exhibitions throughout the north. In addition, Robert is a well respected contributor to many publications such as *The Manchester Evening News*, *Concept For Living*, *Replay*, and *Barnsley Eye* magazine to name a few.

Serves six
Crab and prawn mix
400g/14oz crab meat (a 50/50 mix of white & brown meat)
1 teaspoon Tabasco sauce
1 teaspoon Henderson's Relish
1 teaspoon chopped flat-leaf parsley
1 tablespoon mayonnaise
juice of one lemon
salt and pepper
100g/3½oz of small cooked prawns
12 cooked king prawns (de-shelled)

Marie Rose sauce
2 tablespoons mayonnaise
1 tablespoon tomato ketchup
½ teaspoon Tabasco sauce

Salad garnish
½ Iceberg lettuce
1 tablespoon mini capers
1 banana shallot (diced)
1 tablespoon mayonnaise
salt and pepper

Garnish
6 pieces of Melba toast
6 prawn crackers
6 lemon wedges
6 sun-blessed tomatoes
6 sprigs flat-leaf parsley

Make the Marie Rose sauce by emptying the mayonnaise, ketchup and Tabasco sauce into a bowl and mixing together. Mix together the crab meat, small cooked prawns, Tabasco sauce, Henderson's Relish, mayonnaise, lemon juice and flat-leaf parsley into a separate bowl, adding seasoning to taste.

In a third bowl, mix the lettuce, capers, shallot and mayonnaise, seasoning to taste.

To serve, make a line of Marie Rose sauce at the top and bottom of the plate. Place a ring on the left hand side of the plate and fill it with the crab mix, then remove the ring and place a piece of Melba toast on top. Next to the crab mix, put the lettuce garnish into a ring and place a prawn cracker on top, remove the ring and place two cooked king prawns on top. Finish the plate by garnishing with the sun-blessed tomato, lemon wedge and flat-leaf parsley.

Yarmouth Kipper Paste

Richard Hughes, of The Lavender House, Brundall in Norfolk, has this to say on the subject of his recipe for Yarmouth Kipper Paste:

Whilst looking through my old notes, dating back to the late 1970s, I discovered this gem, made it to go on toast for canapés, and am now munching it on a daily basis. For years we gave a pot of this paste, along with the onion jam, as a Christmas present for my late father-in-law. He always said it was the best present he ever received!

Makes 6 ramekins
2 large kippers
100g/3½oz cream cheese
1 dessertspoon tomato ketchup
pinch of curry spice
juice and zest of 1 lemon
freshly milled black pepper
100g/3½oz celery, peeled and diced
100g/3½oz cucumber, seeds removed, peeled and diced
2 tomatoes, seeds removed and diced

Boil a kettle; pour the water over the kippers, and leave to stand for 5 minutes. Drain the kippers, and discard the liquid. Pick the bones from the kippers; skin and remove the heads. Don't worry too much about all the little 'pin bones' – these will be blended in the food processor.

Place the picked kipper flesh in a food processor. Purée for 2 minutes; scrape the sides of the processor down, and purée again for 1 further minute. The mixture should be smooth, like a fish paste.

Place the kipper paste into a bowl; beat in the cream cheese, the juice and zest of a lemon. Also, the tomato ketchup and the curry spice. Season well with the freshly milled pepper before folding in the diced celery, cucumber and tomatoes. Finally, spoon into ramekins or glass jars, and serve with granary toast.

Yarmouth Kipper Paste. (Photo: Richard Hughes at The Lavender House)

Fresh Morston Mussels

A local Norfolk old-fashioned recipe, which is traditionally cooked whilst the fishing crew is still on the boat. This recipe comes from Jane Robins.

1.75kg/4lb fresh Morston mussels, washed and de-bearded

For the batter mix
125g/4½oz flour
¼ level teaspoon salt
1 egg
300ml/10fl oz milk

Bring a pan of salted water to the boil and throw in the mussels; they should open immediately, in which case they are cooked enough. Remove from water and pull them from their shells before allowing to cool.

Make a batter mix either from the ingredients above or, for a lighter batter, just use flour, water and ice cubes. Coat the mussels with the batter and toss them into hot fat, cooking until golden-brown. Serve with lemon wedges and brown bread.

Colchester Oysters in a Chablis Sauce

It is said that oysters were one of the main reasons for the Roman invasion of these shores. While this may be something of an exaggeration, we do know that the Romans enjoyed enormous quantities of British oysters and that the precious molluscs were exported in large quantities back to Italy. Once plentiful around the UK coastline, native oysters were seriously over-harvested during the late 19th century and, as a result, became the expensive luxury they are today. When buying oysters, make sure that the shells are firmly shut. If any shells are open slightly, tap sharply. Any that do not close immediately should be discarded. Although best eaten on the day of purchase, oysters will keep for 5–7 days if properly stored. They should be kept cool and loosely covered with a damp cloth or seaweed in the bottom of the fridge, with the flat shell uppermost to retain the juices.

Serves six
24 oysters in their shells
1 bottle Chablis
6 rounds wholemeal bread, lightly toasted
3 tablespoons olive oil
55g/2oz butter (unsalted)
6 eggs, beaten
1 tablespoon fresh parsley, chopped
pinch of sea salt
cayenne pepper
parsley sprigs to garnish

Open the oysters and pour their juices into a small pan, together with approximately 6 tablespoons of wine. Heat and reduce until only about 6 tablespoons of liquor remains. Fry the rounds of wholemeal toast in the olive oil until crisp on both sides. Remove from the pan and keep warm. Melt the butter in a saucepan and scramble the eggs until creamy and then mix in the parsley and salt. Drop the oysters into their juice/wine liquor for a few seconds in order to warm them. Place a round of toast in the centre of each serving plate and cover with a portion of the scrambled egg. On top of this, place four oysters and some of the juice. Sprinkle a very small amount of cayenne pepper on top and decorate with sprigs of parsley. The remainder of the bottle of Chablis makes the perfect accompaniment.

Smoked Salmon Salad with a Roasted Lemon and Dill Dressing

The Cottage in the Wood Country House Hotel is independently owned and wonderfully run by the Pattin family. With views to die for, the food matches the view and, in the absence of Dominic Pattin, head chef and director, we were well looked after on the day by Andrew Evans and Maria Taylor who were kind enough to offer five recipes, of which this is the first.

4 slices smoked salmon
4 handfuls mixed salad leaves
cucumber slices
2 lemons
4 sprigs of thyme
1 handful chopped dill
1 egg yolk
25ml/¾fl oz vinegar
1 tablespoon Dijon mustard
olive oil, enough to obtain the required thickness of dressing

To make the lemon and dill dressing, roast off the lemons and thyme for about 1½ hours. Purée the lemons and pass through a sieve and into a bowl. Add the egg yolk, mustard and vinegar, and whisk together slowly whilst adding the olive oil. Season to taste, and mix in the chopped dill.

Add the dressing to salad leaves and sliced cucumber and serve together with the smoked salmon.

Smoked Salmon Salad with a Roasted Lemon and Dill Dressing.

Buttered Morecambe Bay Prawns

Morecambe has always been famous for its prawns and shrimps – to the fishmonger, a prawn is a shrimp bigger than 8cm – use whichever is available.

1ltr/2pt boiled shrimps or prawns
150ml/5fl oz dry white wine
1 teaspoon white wine vinegar
50g/2oz butter
1 level tablespoon plain flour
2 egg yolks
½ teaspoon grated nutmeg
pinch of salt
4 slices bread

Shell and prepare the shrimps by holding the head between the thumb and forefinger of your right hand. Hold the tail with the fingers of your left and gently pinch and pull off the tail shell. Hold the body whilst gently removing the head, soft body shell and small 'claws'. Simmer the shells and other discarded parts in a covered pan for 15 minutes together with the wine, vinegar, salt, nutmeg and enough water to cover. Strain the liquid into a clean pan. Add the shrimp/prawn meat and heat until the liquid is just under boiling point. Mash the butter and flour together and add to the pan a spoonful at a time, stirring constantly. Lightly beat the egg yolks in a small bowl. Add a little of the sauce to them and return this mixture to the rest of the sauce still in the pan. Stir and heat gently until the shrimp/prawn meat is just bound together with a thick, rich sauce.

Toast the slices of bread and cut into triangles; divide the shellfish mixture equally into four ramekin dishes, stand on a plate and place the toast pieces around the base.

Filey Haddock and Crab Fishcakes with Spring Greens and Parsley Veloute

Martin Wilks, owner of Lords Restaurant, Harrogate, North Yorkshire, is a great believer in sourcing local produce:

Sometimes it's easier than others. I can get superb meat and vegetables from nearby Nidderdale, Airedale and Wharfedale, and fish from the east Yorkshire coast, but what I put on the menu is dictated by the seasons and a guaranteed continuity of supplies. It's important to keep things in season. In the spring I might get my asparagus from Leeds and my strawberries from Harrogate, but once they are 'out of season', I change. Yes, it's possible to buy Peruvian asparagus and Spanish strawberries all the year round, but English produce tastes much better and these days, everyone is (or should be) thinking of air miles. Anyway, it pays to take advantage of what's in season locally as, in the end, it almost always works out cheaper.

Filey Haddock and Crab Fishcakes with Spring Greens.

400g/14oz mashed potato
100g/3½oz white crab meat
100g/3½oz smoked haddock
100g/3½oz parsley
50g/2oz dill
1 lemon
1 leek
200g/7oz Savoy cabbage
200g/7oz baby spinach
30g/1oz butter
30g/1oz flour
100ml/3½fl oz fish stock
50ml/2fl oz white wine
50ml/2fl oz double cream
breadcrumbs
2 eggs
plain flour (for adding to the *veloute* mix)
olive oil
sufficient milk to poach the haddock
seasoning

Prepare the *Filey Haddock and Crab Fishcakes* by mixing the mashed potato together with a little of the cream and a generous knob of butter. Poach smoked haddock in milk and then allow to cool before removing the skin. Flake the fish into the prepared mash and add crab meat, together with zest and juice of lemon. Add chopped half the given amount of parsley and all of the dill. Season to taste. Take a 5cm (2in) pastry cutter and use to mould mix into fishcake.

Put fishcakes in fridge to set. Once chilled, beat eggs and place seasoned flour, beaten eggs and breadcrumbs in three separate bowls. Coat each fishcake in the flour, then egg and finally roll in breadcrumbs ensuring an even coating. Deep fry for 5 minutes until golden-brown and place in 160°C (320°F) oven for 10 minutes.

To prepare the *Spring Greens* wash and finely chop the leek and Savoy cabbage. Mix in the spinach. Take a hot frying pan and stir fry the greens in a little oil and butter – without colouring. Season to taste.

Make the *Parsley Veloute* by melting butter in a saucepan and slowly adding flour until a thick paste is reached. Leave on heat for a few seconds to cook out. Slowly add fish stock, whisking all the time to ensure a smooth consistency. Add white wine and whisk in well. Incorporate the remainder of the cream and bring back to boil stirring all the time (By the time you've finished, the consistency should be such that it will coat the back of a spoon). Add the remainder of the chopped parsley and season to taste.

Present to the table by placing the spring greens in the centre of a hot plate and put the fishcakes on top of the greens. Drizzle a little of the *veloute* around edge of greens and garnish with sprigs of dill or parsley.

~ MEATS ~

Although it is almost certainly a fact that people are nowadays eating meat less regularly than they used to, the increase in the availability of good quality, locally produced meat means that 'real meat' – a term nowadays used to signify that which comes from old-fashioned breeds reared by traditional methods – is, or should be, at the forefront of cooking ingredients. Even what is commonly known as 'offal', from which traditional dishes such as black pudding is derived, has an important place in modern-day regional cooking and is being championed by great chefs such as Fergus Henderson.

You might not think it possible to write a flowing essay in praise of some of the less-attractive parts of meat, but Anthony Bourdain managed it in his book *A Cook's Tour* (Bloomsbury, 2001):

> Years ago, when the prevailing wisdom among foodies dictated quaint, tiny, sculpted portions of brightly coloured odd bits – light on the protein and heavy on the veg, Fergus [Henderson] was reveling in pig – pig fat, pig parts, and pig guts – his plates rustic-coloured palettes of browns, beiges, and earth tones – maybe the occasional flash of green – simple, unassuming, unpretentious – and absolutely and unapologetically British.

Goat's Cheese and Black Pudding Fritters with Caramelized Apples

'M J's', a very attractive and modern restaurant attached to the Whitehall Hotel, Darwen, Blackburn, Lancashire, owes much of its reputation to Steve Waters, the head chef. Unlike some who do not like visitors around when they are working, Steve positively encourages the customers to see their meals being created by the inclusion of a 'viewing' space between kitchen and restaurant.

400g/14oz goat's cheese
100g/3½oz black pudding, chopped
500g/1¼lb breadcrumbs
2 apples, cored and six 0.5cm slices taken from each
25g/1oz butter
25g/1oz caster sugar
egg wash
flour, for coating

For the grain mustard dressing
1 dessertspoon whole grain mustard
100ml/3½fl oz white wine vinegar
200ml/7fl oz extra-virgin olive oil

Goat's Cheese and Black Pudding Fritters.

Remove the 'skin' from the goat's cheese, roughly chop it, and beat down in a blender for about 1 minute. Mix in the chopped black pudding until a black-and-white, marbled effect is achieved. Spoon the mixture into small cooking/baking rings or alternatively, place the mixture on a board and cut out circles using a pastry cutter. Remove the circles and coat in flour before dipping in the beaten egg wash and then into the breadcrumbs. Repeat the procedure in order to ensure that none of the contents escape when being fried.

Put the butter in a frying pan and heat until bubbly and golden (not black and burned!). Add the caster sugar and place the apple slices into the caramelized mixture for 1 minute on each side (this can be done the day before if required).

Cook the goat's cheese and black pudding fritters in a deep-fat fryer or, if you don't have such a thing, fry them on both sides in an ordinary frying pan before finishing them off in the oven for 1–2 minutes. Serve as shown in the accompanying photograph, finished off with a grain mustard dressing made by whisking together the mustard, white wine vinegar and olive oil (this dressing will keep in the fridge for a month).

Potted Goosnargh Duck

There are a couple of recipes which use Goosnargh duck in our 'Main Course' chapter: this starter is another result of our travels round the north-west and was suggested by Alice Booth, one of our bed and breakfast hosts.

Makes six ramekins
2 large Goosnargh duck legs
125g/4½oz Goosnargh duck breast
125g/4½oz Harome chicken breast
500g/1¼lb clarified butter
4 cloves garlic, crushed
small handful of fresh thyme
small handful fresh parsley, finely chopped
salt and pepper

To smoke the duck and chicken breasts
1 level tablespoon rice
1 level tablespoon brown sugar
1 level tablespoon tea leaves
1 lemon or lime, finely sliced

Place the duck legs, butter, garlic, thyme, salt and pepper into a roasting pot, cover and slowly bake for 2 hours at 150°C (300°F). At the end of cooking, the meat should just fall off the bone. When cooked, strip the meat and retain the butter mixture.

Line the bottom of a wok with tin foil, making sure you leave enough foil up the sides to protect the sides of your wok. Place the rice, sugar and tea leaves on the foil and then cut another piece of foil to loosely cover them. On this circle of foil, lay the duck and chicken breasts plus a few slices of lemon or lime. If the wok has a lid, cover it now – otherwise use a third piece of foil and fix it so as to form a secure 'lid' through which no smoke can escape. Smoke for 10–15 minutes by placing the wok on a hob. Remove the breasts and finish them off by cooking in a hot oven for a further 5 minutes. Once cooked, finely chop the breasts and add them, together with the shredded leg meat, to the clarified butter you have retained. Mix in the parsley and spoon the mixture into the ramekin dishes before placing in the fridge to set overnight. Serve as a starter with warm toast and a spoonful of *Spiced Pineapple Pickle* (see page192).

Blackfriars Game Terrine

Blackfriars, situated appropriately enough on Friars Street in Newcastle, is the oldest purpose-built restaurant in the UK, with its origins dating back as far as 1239. Today, owner Andy Hook and his team specialize in what he describes as 'classic but gutsy British food using fresh, local and seasonal produce'. Andy is a member of the 'Slow Food' organization, which celebrates the pleasures of the table and appreciates a slow approach towards cooking and eating as opposed to the 'fast food' culture of the last twenty years or so.

Serves four to eight
1kg/2¼lb game meat – pheasant, partridge, rabbit, pigeon, duck or even hare
12 rashers of streaky bacon
500g/1¼lb sausage meat
200g/7oz chopped liver
freshly made breadcrumbs taken from 2 thick slices of bread
2 cloves garlic, chopped
1 egg
1 handful flat-leaf or curly parsley and thyme, chopped and mixed together
a few juniper berries
1 'glug' red wine
1 'glug' brandy (optional)
1 small handful pistachio nuts, crushed
1 handful gherkins
diced and cooked carrots
sea salt and black pepper
a little olive oil (for frying the game meat)

Turn oven to 160°C (320°F). Mix together the sausage meat and livers and add the breadcrumbs, egg, parsley, thyme, the juniper berries and garlic. Add the red wine (and brandy if you want to be extravagant), season with the sea salt and freshly ground black pepper.

Blackfriars Game Terrine. (Photo: Andy Hook at Blackfriars Restaurant)

Mix thoroughly before turning out and rolling into a 'sausage' roughly the same length as your chosen terrine dish. Next, chop and fry the game meat (in batches if necessary) in olive oil until golden-brown. Mix in a bowl with pistachios, cooked carrots and a handful of gherkins.

Line terrine dish with the stretched rashers of streaky bacon and add half the game meat mix, lay the forcemeat sausage down the middle before heaping on remaining game mix. Fold the exposed strips of bacon over the top of the terrine and cover with kitchen foil and terrine dish lid. Place terrine dish in a roasting tin half-filled with hot water and cook in oven for about 1½ hours (ensure it's cooked through).

Press terrine as it cools with a block of snug-fitting wood and a couple of cans of baked-beans and leave overnight until completely cold. To serve the terrine: slice it thickly with a very sharp knife, place on a plate with a few dressed greens and some fruit chutney. Serve with hot toast.

Wiltshire Ham and Watercress Soup

Add a few boiled and shelled river crayfish to this simple recipe – if in season and readily obtainable.

300g/10½oz cooked Wiltshire ham, cut into bite-sized dice
2 medium-sized potatoes; cut into small dice
1 large onion, finely chopped
1¼ltr/2pt chicken or ham stock
2 bunches watercress, very finely chopped
2 tablespoons butter, unsalted
seasoning

Sauté the onion in a tablespoon of butter. Add the ham and potatoes. Cook without browning for 5 minutes and then add the stock. Simmer until the potatoes are tender and add the leaves from the bunches of watercress. Boil gently for a further 2 minutes; season and stir in the second spoonful of butter, plus – if you can get them – the boiled and shelled crayfish.

Ham and Pea Soup

The inclusion of this recipe is personal indulgence, as it is a firm favourite with one of the authors – even to the extent of his family bringing tinned versions when they visit him in France!

1 ham bone, not too carefully cleared of ham!
450g/1lb dried green peas
2 medium onions
2 carrots
1 small turnip
100g/3½oz swede
2ltr/3½pt water
salt and pepper

Soak the peas overnight before draining them and placing, together with all the other ingredients, into a large saucepan. Bring to the boil, cover and simmer for about 2 hours or until the peas are soft. Remove the ham bone and blend the soup until smooth. Reheat, but do not boil (soup should never be boiled once made), immediately prior to serving and garnish with well-fried bacon lardons and/or croutons.

Partridge and Pea Risotto Soup

For a variety of reasons, it is nowadays quite a simple matter to get hold of a brace or two of partridges for use in game cooking, but it has not always been the case. At first, there was only the grey or English partridge (*Perdix perdix*), which survived well with careful management on the majority of low-ground estates, especially those in the eastern counties. However, after the Second World War, as countryside economics went into decline, so too did the fortunes of the wild grey partridge – relying as it does on an abundance of insect larvae with which to feed its young chicks; the introduction of herbicides also did not help. Enter the red-leg or French partridge (*Alectoris rufa*): a bird introduced to this country due to its ability to breed well artificially and be more easily managed on the sporting estate. It is, therefore, the red-leg that appears most regularly at the game dealers. If, however, you ever have the opportunity to purchase grey partridge, do so: the purists think that it is far superior.

250g/9oz cooked partridge breasts, skinned and shredded
350g/12oz frozen peas, defrosted
1ltr/2pt game, chicken or vegetable stock
170g/6oz risotto rice
1 onion, finely chopped
55g/2oz butter
4 tablespoons grated Parmesan
2 tablespoons flat-leaved parsley, chopped
seasoning

Partridge and Pea Risotto Soup.

Cook the onion in butter in a pan for 5 minutes until it starts to soften. In a food processor, purée half of the quantity of peas. Add the risotto rice to the pan and stir to coat in butter. Pour in the stock and add all the peas and partridge meat. Simmer gently without a lid for about 20 minutes before seasoning to taste and scattering with parsley, grated Parmesan and freshly ground black pepper.

Pressed Terrine of Yorkshire Gammon with Fried Ledstone Quail Egg, Spiced Pineapple Pickle, Mustard Seed Dressing

Andrew and Jacquie Pern acquired The Star in June 1996. The inn had been closed for seven months, and much effort and financial investment were needed to turn a derelict property into what is now considered to be amongst the finest of its kind in Yorkshire.

Andrew says that this particular 'starter' is 'a play on the pub grub classic of gammon, egg and pineapple. This pressed ham knuckle terrine, with a gently fried quail egg perched on top and a rich golden chutney spooned around is a firm favourite on the Star Inn menu.' It is, so he assures us, 'great for dinner parties.'

Makes one terrine – approx ten slices
3 ham knuckles
6 bay leaves
1 large onion chopped in half
2 peeled carrots
6 whole cloves
6 black peppercorns

Place in a deep pan, cover with cold water and bring to the boil and simmer for 2½ to 3 hours until tender.

50g/2oz mixed leaves and herbs for garnish
20g/¾oz finely chopped flat parsley
1 quail egg per portion
a drop of olive oil
Sweet Pineapple Pickle
20ml/¾fl oz grain mustard vinaigrette
6 to 8 slices York ham
2 slices soaked leaf gelatine

Pressed Terrine of Yorkshire Gammon with Fried Ledstone Quail Eggs. (Photo: Andrew and Jacquie Pern at The Star Inn)

While the ham knuckles are cooking, line a terrine mould with cling film, then with thin slices of York ham. When the hams are cooked, remove them from the pan and then leave to cool slightly (but, whilst still warm, remove the meat from the bone). Place in a small bowl with the onion, seasoning and flat parsley. Mix and combine thoroughly, then pack into the terrine mould.

Ladle 500ml (16fl oz) of the ham stock into a pan; checking that it is not too salty (if so, dilute stock with water, before taking the 500ml). Warm it gently before adding the gelatine, pour liquid over the ham into the terrine. Overlap the edges of York ham to cover the ham pieces. Cover with cling film; the terrine needs to be quite solid and well-packed. Place in a fridge with a uniform weight on top for even pressing. Leave overnight.

To present the dish, turn out the terrine, unwrap the cling film, then with a sharp knife slice approx. 2cm thick and place in the centre of a cold dinner plate. Shallow-fry the quail eggs in a little olive oil. Spoon three piles of pickle at intervals around the terrine with a little leaf garnish again at intervals between them. Place the egg on top; grind a little black pepper on top, then drizzle the mustard seed dressing around. Serve immediately, together with *Sweet Pineapple Pickle* (*see* page 192).

Grilled Huddersfield Black Pudding and Bacon Salad with Soft Poached Egg, Toasted Pine Nuts and Mustard Dressing

Here's another starter from Lords Restaurant, Harrogate, North Yorkshire (*See also: Filey Haddock and Crab Fishcakes*, page 36). Owner Martin Wilks suggests that the best way of ensuring a good meal is to source good produce:

> Look at a recipe or think up your own ideas and talk to a local supplier. In the summer, if you want trout, look in Yellow Pages and see if there is a trout farm near to you. In the autumn and winter, find a good butcher or game dealer if you're thinking of anything connected with venison or game. We use all local cheeses – with the exception of an odd piece of French Brie – as yet, Yorkshire hasn't, in my opinion, produced a decent Brie!

Martin also believes that not enough people take advantage of food found in the wild:

> In spring, use the shoots and flowers of wild garlic rather than cloves of the 'shop' variety – it adds a fresher, cleaner taste. Use it mixed with spinach so that it doesn't overpower the delicate taste of dishes such as fish. People should be proud of what their immediate locality has to offer.

Grilled Huddersfield Black Pudding and Bacon Salad.

400g/14oz black pudding, diced
8 slices smoked streaky bacon
4 eggs
1 curly endive lettuce or mixed salad leaves
1 tomato
12 chives
50g/2oz toasted pine nuts
1 teaspoon coarse-grain mustard
1 teaspoon honey
1 tablespoon white wine vinegar
100ml/3½fl oz olive oil/rapeseed oil
salt and black pepper

Grill the bacon until crisp. Grill the black pudding. Toast pine nuts in a hot frying pan until they are golden-brown (this takes seconds, rather than minutes). Place tomato in boiling water for 20 seconds and then plunge into iced water in order to remove the skin. Cut into quarters, remove the seeds and dice the quarters. Poach eggs in boiling water until soft.

To make the *Mustard Dressing*, place mustard, honey and vinegar in mixing bowl and season with salt and black pepper before slowly whisking in the olive or rapeseed oil.

Serve by placing the black pudding on a warm plate together with the bacon and tomato. Place poached egg on top and carefully position a 'ball' of lettuce on top of the egg. Scatter dish with pine nuts, drizzle a little of the mustard dressing over and garnish with whole chives.

~ Vegetarian ~

Even dyed-in-the-wool meat eaters can enjoy a vegetarian meal on occasions; while for others, vegetarianism might be a medical requirement or simply a matter of personal choice. Whatever the reasons, there is no longer the need to think of anything without meat or fish as being boring and restricted to quiches, salads and omelettes.

Good vegetables are (or should be) at the heart of every kitchen and it is important to remember the generally accepted advice to eat 'five portions a day'. Locally grown vegetables are, without doubt, more nutritious than those that have been flown in from another country. Those which are imported are often harvested before they are ripe and are kept in cold storage – resulting in produce that never has chance to develop the flavours and nutritional value of those which have been allowed to ripen naturally and have travelled no further than to your local farmers' market or been delivered to your door by the nearest producer who operates a box scheme.

Beryl's Chilled Cucumber and Avocado Soup

A favourite of Beryl Woodhouse, Staffordshire, with whom we stayed as part of the 'Farm Stay UK' bed and breakfast scheme. Beryl quite rightly points out that avocados are not regionally produced, but excused herself by saying that it's a good way of using up the cucumbers her husband grows in his greenhouse each year!

Serves eight
2–3 ripe avocados
½ large cucumber, roughly chopped
300ml/10fl oz Greek yoghurt
600ml/1pt vegetable stock
60ml/2fl oz lime juice
1 teaspoon 'Lazy Garlic'
1 teaspoon chilli powder
salt and pepper

Peel the avocados and place in a blender together with the cucumber pieces. Process until smooth, and then turn into a large mixing bowl, adding all the other ingredients at the same time. Mix well, taste and season further if necessary. Chill in the fridge for at least 1 hour before serving and garnish with slices of (locally grown!) cucumber or sprigs of watercress.

Alresford Watercress Soup

Just as Wakefield, Yorkshire, is the home of rhubarb growers, Alresford, Hampshire, is the epicentre of British watercress culture. Along the Itchen Valley (amongst other places), one cannot travel for too many miles before coming across watercress beds and, quite often, a farm shop selling both watercress soup and all manner of local produce. Whether you buy the soup ready-made, or bunches of watercress to make your own, it is a delightful, creamy starter or lunchtime snack.

2 bunches watercress
1 onion, chopped
1 potato, diced
25g/1oz butter
450ml/16fl oz milk
300ml/10fl oz vegetarian stock
seasoning

Shred the watercress leaves from the stalk, leaving just a few for garnish. Using a large, heavy-bottomed saucepan, fry the vegetables gently in butter for 5 minutes without burning. Add the milk and stock, and bring to the boil, stirring continuously. Turn the heat down, cover the pan and simmer for a further 15 minutes. Whiz the soup in the blender, or push through a sieve before returning to the pan. Season and reheat. Serve into individual soup bowls, whirl in a spoonful of double cream if desired, and garnish with the remaining watercress leaves.

Watercress beds in the Itchen Valley, Hampshire.

Parsnip and Honey Soup

Chris Birch combines two extremely successful careers in very different spheres. He is both a chef at Frensham, Surrey, and a well-known competition cyclist in the UK and Europe. Wearing his chef's hat, he tells us that this 'very simple soup is perfect for vegetarians and coeliacs.'

Serves six
4 large parsnips, diced
1 small onion, diced
60g/2oz butter
2 vegetable stock cubes
1 tablespoon clear honey
2ltr/3½pt boiling water
seasoning

Melt the butter in a large saucepan and add the onion and parsnips. Cook for a few minutes without allowing it to colour. Mix the stock cubes with the boiling water and add the stock, together with the honey, to the parsnips and simmer for 1½–2 hours. Blend, check the seasoning and serve immediately.

Stilton and Onion Soup

When serving soup as a starter, remember that too large a bowlful can take the edge off even the heartiest of appetites. This is especially true of this particular recipe.

8 medium-sized onions, peeled and chopped
100g/3½oz butter
100g/3½oz Stilton, chopped
1ltr/2pt vegetable stock
1 large glass of white wine
pinch of fresh thyme
salt and freshly ground pepper

Gently melt the butter in a heavy-bottomed saucepan and sauté the onions without burning. Season with salt and pepper. Add the vegetable stock and thyme and bring to the boil. Cover and simmer. After 15 minutes, add the chopped Stilton. After a further 10 minutes, pour in the glass of wine and continue to simmer for 10 minutes more. Serve with croutons and/or crusty bread.

Blackfriars Roasted Butternut Squash Soup. (Photo: Andy Hook at Blackfriars Restaurant)

Blackfriars Roasted Butternut Squash Soup

Andy Hook, owner of Blackfriars Restaurant in Newcastle, can often be seen at North Shield's Fish Quay, Grainger Market and at any farmers' markets he can find. By his own admission, Andy spends 'ridiculous amounts of time researching, sourcing and cooking food.' He will only ever use food when it is in season and organic wherever possible.

1 butternut squash, halved and with the seeds removed
2 red peppers
1 medium-sized onion, chopped
3 cloves garlic, chopped
1 tablespoon honey
75ml/2½fl oz olive oil
175ml/6fl oz glass white wine
500ml/16fl oz vegetable stock
1 level dessertspoon caraway and fennel seeds, mixed
50g/2oz bag pine nuts
1 handful flat-leaved parsley and basil, chopped and mixed
sea salt and black pepper

Pre-heat oven to 180°C (355°F). Place the halved butternut squash onto a baking tray and drizzle with some honey and about a quarter of the olive oil; place in the oven to roast for 30–40 minutes until tender (don't burn!). Gently dry-fry the caraway and fennel seeds, add a little of the remaining olive oil together with the onion and cloves of garlic, and cook until tender. Deglaze with a small glass of white wine and add stock before bringing to the boil. Turn down to a simmer for 10 minutes and then add the cooked squash. Blend using more or less stock (or you could use single cream for luxury) to your required consistency.

Dry roast the pine nuts until golden (reserve a few for garnish); chop a handful of flat-leaf parsley and basil and blend in food processor with the half of the olive oil still remaining, until a smooth pesto paste is achieved.

Oven-roast a couple of red peppers in oven until blackened, cool in sealed bag, peel, de-seed and blend into a *coulis*, at the same time adding the last of the oil and any roasting juices. Sieve carefully in order to remove any lumps. Reheat soup, season to taste with sea salt and freshly ground pepper, pour into bowls, drizzle with red pepper *coulis* (use a cocktail stick to make pretty patterns if desired), spoon pesto into centre, garnish with remaining pine nuts. Serve with hot crusty bread.

West Country Pumpkin Ale Soup

Dorset brewer Hall and Woodhouse, an independent firm founded in 1777, had the bright idea of recently launching two bottled beers specifically aimed at the country-living 'real ale' enthusiast. One, known as 'Poacher's Choice', is a liquorice and damson flavoured beer, which, so the brewer says, 'goes well with desserts and mature cheeses'. The other, 'Pumpkin Ale', has 'hints of roast pumpkin, cloves and peat, is sweet and slightly smoky, and is ideal to drink with sticky toffee apples and carrot cake'. On the back label of each bottle is this recipe for Pumpkin Ale Soup – an ideal autumn or winter starter for a main meal or as a filling lunchtime bowl accompanied by a chunk of warm crusty bread.

1 pumpkin, skin removed and cubed
1 large potato, peeled and cubed
1 onion, chopped
1 small chilli, chopped
2 garlic cloves, peeled and chopped
500ml/16fl oz vegetable stock
1 large wine glass Badger Pumpkin Ale
1 teaspoon curry powder
1 bay leaf
a little butter, to sweat onions
glug of double cream
seasoning

Take the pumpkin flesh, peeled potato and bay leaf, and boil until tender and then drain. Sweat the onion, garlic cloves, chopped chilli and curry powder in a large pan. Add the pumpkin mixture, vegetable stock and ale, simmer and season to taste. Blend to a creamy consistency, add a swirl of double cream, and serve.

Sarah's Courgette Soup

Sarah Rant is Scottish by birth but now lives in France. With recipes to die for (well and truly tested on one of the authors of this book), she combines vegetarian cooking with both her Scottish upbringing and fresh produce from the local markets.

6 fresh courgettes, diced
3 medium-sized onions, chopped
3–4 garlic cloves, peeled and chopped
2 stock cubes ('Kallo' organic vegetable)
1ltr/2pt milk
cream or crème fraîche, to decorate
salt and pepper, to taste

Sweat the onions and garlic for 3–4 minutes. Add the milk and the stock cubes, courgettes, salt and pepper. Simmer for 30 minutes and allow to cool slightly before adding a dollop of cream or crème fraîche. Blend and serve immediately.

Sarah's Celeriac Soup

This is another of Sarah Rant's recipes (see also Sarah's Courgette Soup). As the celeriac and onions come from her husband's garden, you cannot get much more locally sourced than that!

4 large (or 6 medium) onions, chopped into small pieces
1 celeriac, peeled and cut into small cubes
3 vegetable stock cubes
900ml/1½pt milk, semi-skimmed
2 tablespoons olive oil
salt and pepper

Heat the olive oil and add the onion pieces, sautéing for approximately 5 minutes until they are soft and translucent, but not browned. Add the milk and the stock cubes, then add the celeriac pieces. Season with salt and pepper to taste and simmer for 30 minutes. Test and add more seasoning if required. Cool the soup before finally blending in a food processor.

PREPARING LEEKS

Bryan and Susan Webb, proprietors of Darleys' Restaurant, Llandrillo, Corwen, Denbighshire, write:

Everyone knows about leeks and the Welsh on St David's Day; rugby matches and Max Boyce. Leeks are also reputed to be the Queen's favourite vegetable, but how many of us use them at home? The leek is a member of the garlic and onion family, and is grown for its blanched, white stem. In the market, leeks are usually found with their roots and most of their long, strap-like leaves still attached.

One thing that always amazes us is that so few people know how to clean a leek: trim off about an inch of the green top and pull off one outer layer of leaves. Then make a cut the whole length of the leek from the root to the top, turn it 90 degrees and repeat before then placing it under a tap of running cold water in order to remove all the dirt. Shake dry and cut it to the size you want, or leave whole.

People also tend to over-cook leeks, which makes them slimy, but treated with care, leeks are wonderful. In France they call them 'poor man's asparagus'. If you have small baby leeks you can steam or brush with olive oil and grill them, and serve them warm or at room temperature with some grated hard-boiled eggs and vinaigrette. We use leeks in soups such as vichyssoise, leek and bacon, stocks, little tarts with laver bread for canapés and in Darley's Leek Risotto, the recipe for which follows.

Bland to look at when growing, leeks are, nevertheless, the basis of many varied and interesting country recipes.

Darley's Leek Risotto

Do not be afraid of making risotto for dinner parties: you don't have to spend all your time in the kitchen stirring and watching it cook whilst everyone else is sipping their drinks; if you use this method, it can be cooked hours before and reheated successfully. Not only good as a vegetarian starter, it goes well served under grilled fish as a main course.

100g/3½oz unsalted butter
2 leeks cleaned as above and finely cut
4 shallots finely chopped
150g/5oz risotto rice, Carnaroli or Arborio
500ml/16fl oz vegetable stock
25g/1oz Parmesan (more if you like)
3 tablespoons cream
salt and pepper

Melt half of the butter in a sauce pan; add the leeks, season with salt and pepper, cook until soft. Place in a bowl. In a clean saucepan melt the remaining butter, add the shallots and cook until soft for about 5 minutes but do not colour. Add the rice and continue to cook gently for another 3–4 minutes. Season the rice with salt and pepper.

Add half of the stock, bring to the boil, stirring all the time, then turn down the heat. When the rice has absorbed the stock check the texture of the rice to see if it will need more stock, but now it's up to you how much – it depends how much bite you want in the rice, but we would normally add all the remaining stock. The whole operation from raw will take 35 minutes. It's ready when the rice grains are just cooked, but still a little firm.

Tip the risotto into a deep tray, cover with cling film and leave to cool. Refrigerate if you are going to leave it a few hours. When you are ready to serve, put the leeks in a saucepan with a little stock if you have some left or water if not; add this to the risotto, stir until the risotto is hot, add as much Parmesan as you wish and also include the cream at this point (do not put back on the heat). Serve in a deep plate with shaved truffles if available.

In the market, leeks are found with most of their long, strap-like leaves still attached.

Sand Hutton Asparagus and Wild Garlic Risotto

From all our travelling around Britain in search of recipes for inclusion in this book, both the authors think that this one, supplied and cooked by James Brown at The Ivy, The Grange Hotel, Clifton near York, just has to be one of the tastiest. Wild garlic is, of course, seasonal and is normally at its best in early May. One of James' chefs has located patches of it in woods nearby where he walks to work and brings it in daily – you cannot get much fresher or more local than that!

To make acid butter
1 shallot, sliced
100ml/3½fl oz white wine
75ml/2½fl oz white wine vinegar
1 tablespoon double cream
375g/13¼oz butter, cold

Add the shallot, white wine and vinegar to a pan and reduce. Once reduced, add cream.

Over a low heat, slowly stir in the cold butter until it is all incorporated together in the pan. Pass through a strainer into a plastic container with an airtight lid and put in the fridge. If this is kept in the fridge, it will last a month.

For the risotto
200g/7oz Canarolli risotto rice
1 bunch fresh local asparagus
75g/3oz butter
150ml/5fl oz white wine
vegetable stock, hot
3 finely diced shallots
12 leaves wild garlic, handpicked in your local woods
1 dessert spoon acid butter (*see* above)
100g/3½oz Parmesan, grated
salt and pepper

Trim the leaves from the asparagus and remove the bottom inch or so that is hard and pale. Slice the spears but leave the top 2 inches of the spear whole. Blanch the spears and slices separately in salted boiling water and refresh in iced water.

Finely dice the shallots and melt the butter in a heavy-bottomed pan before adding the shallots and sweating until translucent and without colour. Add the rice and cook for 2 minutes, always stirring. Add the wine and keep stirring until it is all absorbed. Slowly incorporate the hot stock a little at a time. Keep stirring! (It is important to keep stirring as the stock is being absorbed in order to release the starch from the grains, making the risotto creamier). After 15–17 minutes the rice should be cooked and have the texture of a peanut. Add the grated Parmesan and the sliced asparagus, keeping the spears for garnish.

Add the acid butter and stir in. At the last possible minute, finely cut the wild garlic and add to the risotto. Season and garnish with asparagus spears and wild garlic flowers.

Sand Hutton Asparagus and Wild Garlic Risotto.

Eggs and Asparagus

Steaming is the classic method of preparing asparagus – it is then served hot with melted butter or cold with an oil and vinegar dressing. There are other recipes, soup, soufflés and the like, but for a simple starter try this one adapted from *A Small Country Kitchen*, a book written in 1932 and now sadly unobtainable.

Serves two
12 stalks asparagus
4 eggs, beaten
40g/1½oz butter
salt and freshly ground pepper
2 slices of bread, toasted

Wash the asparagus in cold water and cut off the woody parts from the base of the stalks. Using a sharp knife, scrape the white part of the stalks downwards. Tie into a bundle that will stand upright. Put salted water to boil in a deep pan and plunge the asparagus stalks upright into the water – making sure that the level comes just below the heads. Cover the pan and boil for 15–20 minutes, or until tender when pierced at the stalk end with the tip of a sharp knife. Drain, refresh briefly under cold running water and drain again.

Cut the tender parts of the asparagus into short lengths of about 1.5cm (½in). Discard the tougher parts. Stir the asparagus pieces into the beaten eggs in a bowl, and season to taste. Butter the toast with a third of the butter and keep warm under the grill. Meanwhile, melt the remainder of the butter in a small heavy-bottomed saucepan and pour in the egg/asparagus mixture, stirring continuously with a wooden spoon until it begins to thicken to a creamy consistency. Divide the mixture between the two slices of toast and serve immediately.

Wild Mushroom Pithivier

The best way to describe a 'pithivier' is as a little pastry case, egg-washed and baked until golden. This vegetarian starter from Sarah and Chris Whitehead and their head chef Jonathan Waters at Whites at the Clockhouse, Tenbury Wells, Worcestershire, is made in a ladle and uses wild mushrooms when in season and is, for this reason, a real autumn treat.

For the ruff puff pastry
115g/4oz strong white bread flour
85g/3oz butter
1 pinch each of sea salt and ground white pepper
1 tablespoon lemon juice
75ml/2½fl oz cold water

Sieve the flour into a bowl and add the salt and pepper. Cut the butter into small cubes and lightly mix into the flour *without rubbing in*. Make a well in the centre; add the lemon juice and enough water to mix the flour into a stiff dough. Turn the dough out on to a well floured surface and roll into an oblong, keeping the sides square. Make one double turn (fold the oblong into three sections to create air pockets). Place in the fridge and leave to rest for 30 minutes. Repeat the rolling, folding and resting process twice more.

For the mushroom filling
60g/2oz butter
3 shallots, peeled and finely diced
3 cloves garlic, peeled and finely diced
340g/12oz fresh mixed wild mushrooms, washed and roughly chopped
1 tablespoon fresh tarragon, chopped
125ml/4fl oz double cream
1 egg, beaten
sea salt and black pepper

Melt the butter in a pan and add the shallots and garlic. Cook over a low heat until soft and then add the mushrooms: cook over a low heat for 3–4 minutes until soft. Add the tarragon and double cream; simmer until the liquid has evaporated, giving a stiff consistency. Season and chill.

Wild Mushroom Pithivier.

To make the pithivier

Ensure the pastry is well rested and the filling is cool. Gently roll out the pastry, carefully ensuring to keep the air between the layers until 0.5cm thick. Cut out four pastry circles approximately 9cm diameter. Place a circle into a lightly floured (60ml/2fl oz) ladle. Place enough of the mushroom filling into the pastry-lined ladle to just under full. Ensure the mixture is pushed in firmly. With the left-over pastry, roll out and cut smaller circles of approximately 7cm in diameter to make the base. Place a base of pastry onto the mushroom filling and seal with the beaten egg – ensuring the edges are well sealed to the base. Turn out and repeat for the remaining three pithivier. Rest in the fridge for 10 minutes. Place on a lined baking sheet, egg wash the top of the pithivier and place in a pre-heated oven at 200°C (390°F) for 20–30 minutes until light golden and crisp.

For the sauce
1 shallot, peeled and roughly diced
1 tablespoon olive oil
3 large sprigs fresh tarragon
300ml/10fl oz red wine
300ml/10fl oz vegetable stock
1 dessertspoon redcurrant jelly
sea salt and ground black pepper

Add the olive oil to a stainless steel pan and sauté the shallot. Add the red wine and tarragon and reduce the liquid by half. Add the vegetable stock and redcurrant jelly; again reduce by half or until the required consistency is reached. Season and strain through a fine sieve.

To serve, put a small amount of the sauce in the bottom of a bowl/serving dish and place the pithivier on top. Serve immediately.

Baked Cheesecake of Watercress and Goat's Cheese

A recipe created by Ernst Van Zyle, the head chef at Stanneylands Hotel, Wilmslow, Cheshire.

Makes six
500g/1lb soft cream cheese
250g/9oz soft goat's cheese
4 whole eggs, lightly beaten
1 egg yolk
35g/1¼oz watercress, washed and finely chopped
salt and pepper

Baked Cheesecake of Watercress and Goat's Cheese.

Pre-heat oven to 150°C (300°F) before creaming together the cheeses. Slowly work in the lightly beaten whole eggs and egg yolk; stir in chopped watercress and season to taste. Line the bottom of each of six 7.5cm-diameter metal rings, firstly with cling-film and then with tinfoil and place on a baking tray. Spoon the cheesecake mixture into the rings, almost, but not quite, to the top. Bake in pre-heated oven for 12–15 minutes until set. Allow to cool before removing the cheesecakes from the rings.

To serve, reheat cheesecakes for 2 minutes in a hot oven and serve alongside a garnish of dressed watercress leaves.

Potted Cheshire Cheese

Potted cheese can be easily made from fresh, or even leftover, cheese, and is delicious on toast as a starter. It can also be used as a very tasty sandwich filling.

Makes four ramekins
450g/1lb Cheshire cheese
75g/3oz unsalted butter
1 teaspoon mustard powder
50g/2oz clarified butter
60ml/2fl oz dry sherry (optional variation)
pinch of ground mace (optional variation)

Make the clarified butter by placing unsalted butter in a heavy-bottomed saucepan and melting over a very low heat, taking great care not to brown it. The sediment will eventually settle at the bottom of the pan, at which time remove from the heat and strain the butter liquid through muslin. Leave to cool, but not solidify, before using to pour over. Grate the cheese and fork it into the butter and the teaspoon of mustard powder. Mash it together, pack it tightly into the ramekin dishes and cover with the clarified butter.

Give a totally fresh dimension to this traditional English dish by using the same quantities of cheese and butter and seasoning with a pinch of ground mace, together with the dry sherry.

James' English Salad.

James' English Salad

James Holah is a dynamic young chef who trained in some of London's top restaurants, alongside the likes of Gordon Ramsey and Marco Pierre White. He is currently working in glorious Lancashire countryside and remarks that,

London chefs work differently to country chefs. Out in the countryside, inspiration comes from the fresh produce available and I am fortunate in being given free rein to work on recipes with an emphasis on fresh, regional and seasonal. It's OK to refine a basic product, but don't 'fuss' it up – the ingredients should be the star of the show.

1 English Gem lettuce
6 small cherry or plum tomatoes, halved
cucumber, sliced
6 small fresh spring onions, cut into three
12 radishes, washed, sliced and placed into cold water for 30 minutes in order to crisp
4 large eggs placed in cold water, brought to the boil and cooked for 5 minutes (refresh them under cold running water for 3 minutes), peeled and cut into quarters

For the salad cream
6 hard-boiled eggs, separated, the yolks sieved into a bowl, the whites
coarsely chopped
2 teaspoons sugar
salt and cayenne pepper
2 rounded teaspoons dry English mustard
1½ tablespoons tarragon vinegar
1 tablespoon fresh tarragon, finely chopped
275ml/9¾fl oz double cream

To make the dressing, whisk together the egg yolks, sugar and seasoning, mustard and vinegar. Add the tarragon, chopped egg whites and cream and mix thoroughly.

Scatter the lettuce on plates, followed by the egg, tomatoes, onions, radishes and cucumber. Drizzle the salad cream over and serve.

NOTE: James says that adding anchovy fillets, as illustrated here, makes an interesting non-vegetarian 'starter'.

Warm Asparagus Salad, with Poached Egg and Hollandaise Sauce

This warm salad combines asparagus, potatoes and peppers, and is topped with a soft poached egg. Although suggested here as a starter, it makes the perfect vegetarian supper.

500g/1lb new potatoes, the smaller the better
4 large eggs
125g/4½oz jar of roasted red peppers, drained and chopped
2 bunches asparagus
2 tablespoons olive oil
½ teaspoon smoked paprika
4 tablespoons Hollandaise sauce

Boil the potatoes in traditional fashion before draining and cutting into thick slices. Combine half of the olive oil with the paprika and, in a bowl, mix together with the potatoes until they are thoroughly coated. Heat the remaining oil in a frying pan or wok and add the spears of the asparagus; cook for about 5 minutes or until they are just slightly charred-looking and tender. Remove from the pan and set aside to keep warm. In the same pan, fry the potato slices before adding them to the asparagus spears. Add the peppers to the pan, cooking just long enough for them to heat through. Tip into the potatoes and asparagus.

Poach the eggs and remove to drain on kitchen roll. Split the potato/asparagus mixture between four serving plates and top off each with a poached egg, together with a tablespoon of Hollandaise sauce. Serve with warmed toast.

Fanny Watson's Locally Grown Radish and Cucumber Salad

Ideal as either a starter or a side salad to accompany other dishes, Fanny also suggests using radishes in salsas and stir-fries and offers the following storage advice: 'Although the radish bunches look very pretty with their leaves on, to avoid moisture and nutrient loss, remove the leaves from radish bulbs before storing them in the fridge.'

8–10 radishes, finely sliced
1 large cucumber, finely sliced
2–3 spring onions, sliced
1 clove garlic, crushed
small handful fresh mint leaves
small handful coriander leaves
1 teaspoon sugar
salt and freshly ground black pepper, to taste

Combine the ingredients in a salad bowl and mix thoroughly.

For the dressing
50ml/2fl oz olive oil
50ml/2fl oz white wine vinegar
juice of half a lime

Combine the olive oil and vinegar and mix into the salad. Drizzle with the lime juice to serve.

The Main Course

If a starter gives you the opportunity to begin to think imaginatively, then the main course should be a 'no holds barred' blank canvas as far as creativity is concerned. The pleasure of eating doesn't just begin when we sit at the table. There is the anticipation of the menu, both in its invention, its preparation and in its eventual tasting. A meal begins with preparation – who has not suddenly felt hungry upon entering a kitchen and smelling onions and garlic being fried gently in butter? Perhaps, however, of all the senses, it is sight that provides the biggest 'turn on' – at least until such time as we can actually get to taste what is on the plate.

When planning a main course, always try to imagine the colours of everything on the plate before making a decision as to what combinations of fish, fowl or meat will work best visually and as a marriage of tastes. For the same reason, take some time in choosing what crockery complements your intended menu; too rich and deep a pattern can often swamp the colours of the meal. Size matters, too: a vast array of food cramped on a small plate can be over-bearing and is certainly not as visually attractive – no matter how spectacular its contents are to taste.

~ Fish ~

Fish is one of the most important sources of protein in our diet, rich in minerals such as calcium, phosphorus and iron. In addition, saltwater fish contain all-important iodine. Thirty years ago, the recipe books were decrying the fact that most of the day-to-day food shopping was done at the supermarket and that there was a noticeable decline in the numbers of privately owned fish shops to be found in towns and villages. Thankfully, some of these small outlets are beginning to re-emerge and, depending on your location, it should be once again possible to buy all manner of locally caught fish, both fresh- and seawater. The opportunity to buy from a farmers' market or local supplier should not be missed, both from the point of there being many traditional and extremely interesting recipes and the fact that it is possible to buy the heads, bones and trimmings of some fish species – all of which are important ingredients to stocks and *bouillons*.

Wild Sea Bass with Sweet Red Onion Mashed Potato, Confit Fennel and Baby Calamari with Liquorice-Cream Sauce

The Great House Hotel, Laleston, Bridgend, South Wales, is the home of Leicester's Restaurant and is owned by Norma and Stephen Bond who restored the building from a derelict shell in 1986. As owner, Stephen is also 'Lord of the Manor of Laleston' and, in keeping with the history of the place (the original house is believed to have been a gift from Queen Elizabeth I to the Earl of Leicester), his food reflects a modern approach to classical cooking.

Serves two
1 sea bass filleted
1 fennel bulb
1 red onion
2 Maris Piper potatoes
50g/2oz butter
1 shallot
30ml/1fl oz white wine
2 sticks liquorice
100ml/3½fl oz fish stock
1 baby squid cleaned and sliced into rings
250ml/8fl oz goose fat
milk
flour
20ml/¾fl oz cream
sprinkle of caster sugar
salt and pepper

Firstly slice the fennel into quarters and place in pan with goose fat. Put on a gentle heat for 2 hours. This can be done the day before.

For the mashed potato; boil the potatoes for approximately 25 minutes, slice the red onion and sauté in a pan with a sprinkle of caster sugar. Drain the potatoes and mash with some butter and milk. Then stir in the red onion before seasoning to taste.

For the calamari squid, soak in some seasoned milk and dip in flour and deep fry for 20 seconds.

For the liquorice sauce, place the liquorice in a pan and cover with water. Bring to the boil and simmer for 5 minutes. Drain and blend the liquorice. In a separate pan, sauté the shallot and white wine, then add the fish stock, liquorice paste and 20ml of cream. Season to taste.

Heat a non-stick frying pan and place the sea bass in, skin side down, for 3–4 minutes. Turn over and take off the heat. Rest for 2 minutes.

Pan-Fried Wild Trout

The most easily available trout is undoubtedly rainbow, no matter whether it be bought from the supermarket or given to you by a friend who enjoys fishing at one of the many trout fisheries throughout the country. Some can be amazingly good, especially when taken from chalk streams or a fishery privileged enough to be served by clear unsullied waters. Others, unfortunately, can taste very muddy and unpleasant when cooked – much depends on their origins and on what they have been feeding.

Nothing, however, can beat the freshly caught and gutted wild brown trout simply pan-fried in butter or wrapped in tinfoil and cooked either in the oven or over the hot coals of a barbeque. Before enclosing in tinfoil, liberally smear the fish with butter and add a squeeze of lime juice. Wild brown trout rarely get too big, but, irrespective of whether it is brown or rainbow being cooked, allow roughly 10 minutes per 450g (1lb) at 180°C (355°F).

Narborough Trout with Cockle & Bacon Salad

Richard Hughes of The Lavender House, Brunall, Norfolk, recalled an unpleasant experience when he let us have his recipe for Narborough Trout:

> The date was 4 July 1977, and my very first task in full time employment was the gutting of slimy fresh trout. As the scissors pierced the eye cavity, a fountain of inky black liquid spurted straight into my face. It was all downhill from there!

Serves two
2 fresh trout, cleaned, filleted and 'pin-boned'
50g/2oz grated mature cheddar cheese
100g/3½oz white bread without crust
25g/1oz butter
chopped parsley and tarragon

Place the bread in a processor, and blend until fine. Add the grated cheese, the butter and the herbs. Blend again. Spread the crumbs onto the flesh of the trout fillets.

Heat a little butter or oil on a grilling tray. Grill the trout fillet, crumb side up until golden-brown. Carefully flip over and grill skin side up for a further 3 minutes.

Narborough Trout with Cockle & Bacon Salad. (Photo: Richard Hughes at The Lavender House)

The salad
a good handful of your favourite lettuce leaves
1 ripe juicy pear, peeled, cored and sliced
2 rashers dry-cured streaky bacon, grilled to a crisp
50g/2oz cockles
juice of 1 lemon
1 dessertspoon light olive oil
1 good handful chopped parsley
salt and pepper

Toss the washed lettuce in the lemon and oil before seasoning with salt and pepper. Finally, mix in the chopped bacon, the pear, the cockles and the parsley.

Seared Organic Salmon with a Fricassee of Summer Vegetables.

Seared Organic Salmon with a Fricassee of Summer Vegetables and Herb Butter

Every chef's dream is to be honoured with a Michelin star. Out of all the restaurant guides, Michelin is the most prestigious for both chef and restaurateur. Michelin trends are constantly changing. Recently the tendency has been to sing the praises of the smaller establishments located in rural areas, serving authentic locally sourced cuisine. Young chefs who find ways of bringing their individual styles into their dishes are also in favour. James Holah's style and enthusiasm should certainly win him a star or two in the near future.

Serves one
1 piece of wild or organic salmon
6 morel mushrooms
1 baby courgette
2 pieces asparagus
4 Jersey Royal potatoes
handful of fresh peas and broad beans
rapeseed oil
chives
chervil
tarragon
dill
mint
225g/8oz butter
1 shallot
1 glass white wine
lemon juice

Make the herb butter by first of all finely chopping all of the herbs except for the chives and mint. Dice the shallot and sweat it in a little of the oil. Deglaze the pan with the white wine and leave to cool. Beat the butter in an electric mixer until pale. Combine all the ingredients so far and roll into a sausage shape with cling film and chill.

Thoroughly wash the potatoes and cook them (still in their skins) in salted water at a simmer and with a sprig of mint. Once tender, drain and leave to steam. Sear the salmon on the skin side until golden-brown, turn, place a slice of the butter on the top and finish off under a hot grill before seasoning with lemon juice.

Slice the courgette and asparagus, shell the peas and beans and wash the morels before placing them all into a small pan containing a little water. Bring to the boil and cook away the water (this should leave you with glazed vegetables, which are just cooked and tender). Halve the Jersey Royals and place in the centre of the serving plate. Put the salmon on top and spoon around the vegetables. Finish with a touch of the rapeseed oil and snipped chives.

Simple Salmon and Samphire

Salmon is such a wonderful fish that its delicate flavour is, to our minds, spoilt by any attempt at adventurous sauces. Can there be anything better than a salmon steak oven-baked in a parcel of tinfoil containing butter and lemon juice and served with new potatoes, or anything more subtle than a terrine? Enhance the salmon's delicate flavour with an accompaniment of samphire – either bought from your local producer or, better still, picked by your own fair hands! It grows on estuaries below the high tide mark and can be eaten raw or boiled and served with butter in the same way as asparagus.

4 salmon steaks (each about 115g/4oz)
225g/8oz samphire
olive oil
30g/1oz butter
caster sugar
salt and freshly ground black pepper

Heat the grill to high and meanwhile bring a large saucepan of water to the boil. Brush the salmon steaks with olive oil before placing them under the grill. Grill both sides. Whilst they are cooking, place the samphire into the boiling water, together with a tablespoon of caster sugar. Boil for only a couple of minutes; drain and incorporate the butter. Shake the pan well so that all the samphire is coated with melted butter before making a 'nest' of samphire on each dining plate and topping with a salmon steak. Season to taste. Serve with new potatoes and a smile!

Salmon Steak with a Vegetable Nage

At the time we visited The Cottage in the Wood at Malvern Wells, Worcestershire, this particular recipe was on the menu as 'Grilled Market Fish of the Day'. Bearing in mind the weather conditions at the time we visited, it could well have swum there on its own!

4 salmon steaks
1 pepper, sliced
4 baby corn cobs, sliced
50g/2oz sugar snap peas, sliced
2 courgettes, sliced
¼ leek, sliced
¼ bunch fresh tarragon, chopped
fish stock
25g/1oz garlic butter

Coat the salmon skin in flour and seasoning before frying, skin-side down until crispy. Turn over and fry again before cooking the fish in the oven for about 8 minutes.

For the vegetable nage, simmer all the remaining ingredients in the resultant fish stock for 15 minutes; when done, add garlic butter to finish and season to taste.

Salmon Steak with a Vegetable Nage.

BASS AND LAVER BREAD

Bass and laver bread has been a favourite of Bryan and Susan Webb of Darleys' Restaurant, Llandrillo, Corwen, Denbighshire, since the early 1980s, when they would seek out fresh sea bass caught along the local coast:

Line-caught and stiff as a board, we would have to leave them a day in order to be able to fillet them.

Bass is the one thing Wales has in common with the south of France, we have the best swimming around our shores and these days farmed bass is readily available for the home cook and restaurants that choose to serve a 'one portion' fish. The wild type is always the first choice. Fresh line-caught bass have a ravishingly beautiful bright silver belly, which darkens to a pale blue grey on its sides. It's a great sporting fish and thrives in rough weather.

Laver bread grows on the rocks and beaches of the Gower coast near Swansea. It has a dark and smooth appearance, which makes it distinctive. Traditionally, it is boiled for hours to render it to a thick purée; it is sold in the markets and fishmongers in South Wales and it's a part of Welsh culture and heritage.

Darleys' Roast Wild Bass with Laver Bread Butter Sauce

The combination of fresh wild bass and a light laver bread butter is a simple combination, but it is a light dish and speaks volumes about Welsh food.

4 x 150g/5oz pieces of wild bass, skin on and all pin bones removed
4 finely chopped shallots
1 tablespoon white wine vinegar
175ml/6fl oz glass dry white wine, Muscadet if possible
250g/9oz unsalted butter
salt and a pinch of cayenne pepper
juice of half a lemon
2 tablespoons Laver bread
2 tablespoons double cream
300g/10½oz raw picked spinach
50g/2oz extra butter
olive oil

Put the white wine, vinegar and shallots into a saucepan and slowly reduce to a syrup.

On a light heat, slowly add the butter a little at a time until it forms a slightly thick sauce, season with salt and cayenne pepper; add the juice of the half lemon. Strain the

Darleys' Roast Wild Bass with Laver Bread Butter Sauce. (Photo: Bryan and Susan Webb at Darleys')

sauce into a clean saucepan. In a separate saucepan add 2 tablespoons of laver bread with 2 tablespoons of cream, bring to the boil and add half the *beurre blanc* created earlier.

Season the fish and coat lightly with olive oil and place onto a hot griddle, skin side down, until the skin is crisp. Place onto an oiled tray and bake in a hot oven at 200°C (390°F) for 5 minutes. While the fish is cooking, in a large pan melt the extra butter and cook the spinach until wilted.

Serve the bass on a bed of spinach and pour the laver bread sauce around one side and the remaining *beurre blanc* around the other side.

Pan-Fried Sea Bass; Baby Gem Lettuce, Pancetta and Baby Onions

Another sea bass recipe comes from Jayne O'Malley, partner in The Town House, Solihull in the Midlands.

2 sea bass (600–800g/1¼lb–1¾lb) filleted, scaled and pin-boned
olive oil
knob of butter
lemon juice

Garnish
4 baby gem hearts
12 peeled baby onions
12 chunks pancetta
12 sprigs chervil
chicken stock

Sauce
250ml/8fl oz white wine
250ml/8fl oz Noilly Prat
4 sliced shallots
4 white peppercorns
2 sprigs thyme
500ml/16fl oz fish stock
500ml/16fl oz double cream
seasoning

Cook the fillets of bass simply in an oven pre-heated to about 220°C (430°F): put a piece of greaseproof paper on the bottom of a baking tray, rubbed with olive oil, and bake for around 12–15 minutes, depending on the thickness of your fish. Alternatively, wrap them in a loose parcel of foil after coating them with oil, a knob of butter and a little lemon juice and cook for a similar amount of time.

To make the sauce, put the wine, Noilly Prat, shallots, pepper and thyme in a pan and reduce until almost all the wine has gone. Add the fish stock and reduce this until 250ml (8fl oz) remains. Add the cream and reduce until the sauce coats the back of a spoon. Season with sea salt to taste before finally passing through a fine sieve.

To make the garnish, wash the lettuce well then pan fry in a little hot oil until the outer leaves are wilted and golden-brown. Cover with chicken stock, season and cook in the oven (turning every 10 minutes) until tender all the way through (approx 30 minutes). Cook the baby onions in chicken stock until tender and pan fry the pancetta in a little oil until golden. Cook the previously baked and part-cooked fish in a hot pan with clarified butter, skin side down until golden-brown (approx 3 minutes) then turn and remove from the heat. Squeeze a little lemon over and some rock salt. Serve by placing the lettuce in the centre of the bowl. Put the onions and bacon around, and the fish on top. Using a hand blender, 'froth' the warmed sauce before spooning a little over and around the fish. Garnish with sprigs of chervil.

Smoked Haddock Rarebit

At The Blackwell Ox, Sutton-on-the-Forest, Yorkshire, it is possible to find this recipe on the menu. It would make a lovely lunchtime snack or a traditional 'high tea' dish, but we have decided to include it here in the 'Main Course' chapter.

4 smoked haddock fillets
700g/1¼lb mature Cheddar cheese
25g/1oz plain flour
50g/2oz fresh breadcrumbs
1 tablespoon English mustard
2 'shakes' of Worcestershire sauce
salt and pepper
milk
2 eggs
2 egg yolks

Smoked Haddock Rarebit.

Slowly melt the cheese in a little milk on a low heat (don't boil it; otherwise the mixture will 'split'). Add the flour, breadcrumbs and mustard. Cook for a few minutes until the mixture begins to leave the sides of the pan. Add the Worcestershire sauce, salt and pepper and leave to cool. When completely cold, place the mixture into a food processor at 'low speed' setting and add the eggs and egg yolks. Chill the mixture for a few hours before use.

Cover the haddock fillets with the mixture and bake in a moderate oven for 5–10 minutes before finally browning off under the grill.

Craster Kipper Kedgeree

Craster kippers are a traditional product of the Northumberland coast and are as famous and popular as those from the Isle of Man.

Serves two
2 Craster kippers
100g/3½oz basmati rice
2 hard-boiled eggs, peeled and quartered
450ml/16fl oz fresh milk
100ml/3½fl oz double cream
seeds of 4 cardamom pods, crushed
2 teaspoons medium curry powder
1 teaspoon brown sugar
1 teaspoon grated ginger
salt
knob of butter for coating the kippers
a few coriander leaves for garnish

Cook the rice and set aside. Bake the two kippers, coated with butter and wrapped in foil until the flesh flakes easily from the bone (about 15 minutes). Reserve the flesh and discard the bones. Heat the milk, double cream, crushed cardamom seeds, curry powder, sugar and ginger. Season with salt. Combine the cream mixture with the rice and fish before placing the hard-boiled eggs on top and finishing with the coriander leaves.

STAR-GAZEY PIE

Traditionally eaten on 23 December, known in Cornwall as 'Tom Bawcock's Eve', Star-Gazey pie is unusual in that it has the heads of fish poking through the pastry. Locals thought that it would be wasteful to cover the inedible heads with pastry, but to save the rich oil they contained, the fish were cooked with their heads poking out of the pie in order that the beneficial juices would then filter back into the base of the pie dish. Nowadays, pilchards are cleaned and boned and their heads cut off. The fish are then laid in a deep dish and covered with milk and a thick pastry crust, after which the heads are pushed into slits cut into the pastry and the tails tucked under the edge before being baked in the oven. This local delicacy is usually served with a sauce of sour cream.

Elsewhere in Britain, the type of fish pie eaten depended on where you lived – which is why there are so many regional variations. For centuries, fish was considered to be a penitential food and it was not until the fifteenth century, when the Church decreed that certain days should be meat-free, that fish became to be considered a meal in its own right. Medieval Britons would often mix fish and fruit. Mackerel and gooseberries were cooked in the same pie, as were cod and pears or crystallized lemon peel. In Yorkshire, apples and potatoes were added to herring pies.

Ginger Beer Batter for the Best Fish 'n' Chips Ever!

Preparing a batter for fish and chips is not the easiest thing in the world – some regular recipes produce a very thick batter that overpowers the taste of the fish and, when using the best locally sourced fish from local coastal waters, what's the point in that? A light batter can be made by using sparkling water, but Vernon Blackmore of The Anchor at Woodbridge, Suffolk, suggests the following.

75ml/2½fl oz real ale
75ml/2½fl oz ginger beer
125g/4½oz plain flour
1 tablespoon olive oil
1 thumb ginger peeled and finely grated
pinch of salt

Mix all the ingredients together and leave to stand for 30 minutes before using it.

~ MEATS ~

The sourcing of any meat is important and not just in connection with quality and pricing: all the chefs we spoke to in connection with this book emphatically believe that the best flavours come from local meats. There was even much discussion regarding the quality of meat from a particular region. For example, Ernst Van Zyl, head chef at Stanneylands Hotel, Wilmslow, Cheshire, was emphatic that the meat from the Herdwick sheep is much leaner than normal lamb and the quality of taste is so much better – which is why he prefers to use it in his recipe for Roasted Best End of Lamb.

Hanging meat is another important issue: meat that has been hung well will be darker in colour, but also, and this is the point of it, more tender and flavoursome. Meat which has been hung for twenty-eight days is highly prized for its flavour and legally, a carcass can be hung for up to four weeks to tenderize. But, and it is an important 'but', it would be impossible for the parts of the carcass that are normally minced to then be sold. Under EU regulations, mince (and this includes that used for sausage-making) cannot be kept by the producer/butcher for longer than six days and because of this, there is inevitably some wastage on a beast that has been hung – sometimes as much as 40 per cent – making the best cuts of meat more expensive than they would be if taken from a freshly killed animal. You do, as they say, 'pays your money and takes your choice'. When buying meat one way of testing whether or not it has hung is to press it firmly with your thumb – if the meat retains the impression, it has hung – if it 'springs' back, it is fresh.

Ribble Valley Lamb Chops
and Morecambe Bay Prawns

Forget all those dubious-sounding 'surf and turf' combinations you might have seen in your local pub. Fish and meat can work together, as this recipe proves!

Serves two
4 lamb chops
2 small onions, chopped
½–1 bottle real ale
1 ramekin potted shrimps
knob of butter

Brown the lamb chops, together with the onions, in a frying pan with the butter, then cover them with a quantity of real ale. Simmer very gently for 1½ hours. Skim off any fat and serve with a spoonful of potted shrimps on top, allowing the butter to melt into the braise. Garnish with chopped parsley and serve with boiled potatoes and green beans.

Ernst Van Zyl uses local lamb in his Roasted Best End of Herdwick Lamb recipe, saying that it is much leaner than any other breeds.

Shelly's Lancashire Hot-Pot

No gastronomic trip to the north-west could be complete without the inclusion of this particular dish! Probably made famous worldwide by constant references to 'Betty's Hot-Pot' in the ITV programme *Coronation Street*, the recipe is generally very traditional and possesses almost mystical qualities. Lest you think this too fanciful, Michelle Butterworth, owner of Shelly's, Warrington, Cheshire, told us of the time when, as a young woman she worried about trying to make one. Seeking advice from her grandfather, he told her, 'Don't worry, you'll just know what to use and how much.' 'Sure enough,' said Michelle, 'when I got pearl barley in my hand, I just *knew* it was the right amount.' Part of Michelle's success in the restaurant may be down to her cooker – an Aga named 'Cromwell' – perfect for the slow cooking of hot-pots, roasts and meringues.

Serves 'an army' – very appropriate bearing in mind it's being cooked
on 'Cromwell'! Make a quantity and freeze it.
1kg/2¼lb diced white onion
2.25kg/5lb diced, lean beef
1kg/2¼lb sliced carrots
1 head celery
1.5kg/3⅓lb diced potatoes
large pinch of mixed herbs
1 dessertspoon tomato purée
1 tablespoon beef bouillon or 2 stock cubes
1 tablespoon (or a 'Michelle' handful!) pearl barley
water

Fry the onions in a heavy casserole-type dish or pan until soft before adding the diced beef. Seal the meat and add a little water. Cook for 10 minutes and then add the carrots, celery, potatoes, beef bouillon, herbs and tomato purée. Leave for a further 10 minutes before adding the pearl barley. Cook in the oven at a medium heat for 1½–2 hours.

NB: Everyone's recipe for this dish is different – which is how a regional adaptation should be. One contact says that it should always be made with mutton, which, according to them, has 'so much more flavour'. Clarissa Dickson-Wright suggests that 'a nice touch is to place a dozen fresh oysters' in the mix.

Shelly's Lancashire Hot-Pot in preparation . . .

. . . and on the table (served here with a 'cobbler' top – see *page 91).*

Cheviotdale Pie

Rather than the conventional pie topping, this adaptation of a traditional regional classic uses a cross between Yorkshire pudding and a suet pastry.

1 tablespoon oil
450g/1lb lean minced lamb
1 large onion, chopped
2 tablespoons dark muscovado sugar
300ml/10fl oz lamb or vegetable stock
4 teaspoons Worcestershire sauce
salt and pepper
225g/8oz self-raising flour
25g/1oz cornflour
75g/3oz shredded suet
300ml/10fl oz milk

Heat the oil in a pan and cook the minced lamb for a few minutes until beginning to brown. Add the onion and continue to cook for another few minutes until soft. Stir in the sugar, stock and Worcestershire sauce. Season and simmer for 20 minutes. Spoon into a 1ltr (2pt) pie dish.

Put the flour, cornflour and suet into a mixing bowl and gradually beat in the milk to form a thick batter. Season with salt and pepper. Spoon the batter over the meat mixture and cook for 30–35 minutes at 180°C (355°F) until the crust is risen and golden.

Herefordshire Fidget Pie

The name of this pie is said to have come from the fact that it was originally 'fitched' or five-sided in shape. However, other suggestions as to the origins of the name seem to veer towards the fact that 'fitchett' was an old country name for apples, which are used in the recipe. Although this is specifically a recipe for 'Herefordshire Fidget Pie', there are similar ones to be found in the Huntingdon and Shropshire regions.

375g/13¼oz dry home-cured bacon, coarsely chopped
1 onion, coarsely chopped
1 cooking apple, peeled and coarsely chopped
2 tablespoons chopped parsley
1 tablespoon cornflour
150ml/5fl oz dry cider
350g/12oz ready-made short-crust pastry
beaten egg, for glazing
salt and pepper

Place the bacon, onion, apple and parsley in a 570ml (1pt) pie dish and mix together. Blend the cornflour with a little of the cider to make a smooth paste. Stir in the remaining cider and season to taste with salt and pepper. Pour into the pie dish.

On a floured surface, roll out the pastry dough. Cut off a long strip to fit round the edge of the pie dish. Brush the rim of the dish with a little water and press the dough strip around it. Brush with water. Place the dough lid on top, trim off the surplus and press the edges together in a fluted pattern. Brush the dough with beaten egg and cut a hole in the middle. From the dough trimmings cut decorative leaves and arrange on top. Brush with beaten egg. Bake in the oven for 45 minutes at 190°C (375°F) or until the pastry is crisp and golden and the filling is cooked.

Braised Devon Roast

Braising is a cooking technique that involves quickly browning meat, before cooking it slowly in the oven in a tightly covered container together with a small amount of liquid.

Serves six
900g/2lb joint silverside of beef
15g/½oz beef dripping
75g/3oz onions, sliced
1 clove garlic, chopped
350g/12oz mushrooms, sliced
300ml/10fl oz strong bitter beer
300ml/10fl oz beef stock
50g/2oz tomato purée
1 tablespoon each of chopped fresh thyme and parsley
salt and pepper

Heat the dripping in a flameproof casserole dish and seal the beef, turning until it is browned but not burnt. Remove and set aside. Reduce the heat before adding the onions and garlic to the casserole dish and cooking until soft (about 5 minutes). Stir in the beer and stock and bring to the boil. Add the tomato purée, thyme, parsley and salt and pepper. Place the meat back in the dish, surround it with mushrooms, cover and cook in the oven at 200°C (390°F) until the meat is tender. Remove, wrap in foil and allow to rest. Meanwhile, simmer the remaining contents of the casserole over a low heat for roughly 10 minutes or until the sauce has reduced by half (skim off any floating fat from the liquid before doing so). To serve, slice the beef and arrange on a warmed serving plate before spooning over the sauce.

Dave Waller's Award-Winning Sausages with Creamed Potatoes, Roast Carrots and Sweet Red Onion Gravy

Dave Waller is one of the local suppliers of produce to the Pattin family at the Cottage in the Wood Country House Hotel at Malvern Wells, Worcestershire.

12 sausages
4 large carrots, sliced into triangle-shaped pieces
½ orange
20g/¾oz butter
seasoning
750g/1½lb potatoes, peeled and cut
seasoning
30g/1oz butter
¼ small nutmeg

To make the gravy
4 red onions, skinned and thinly sliced down the centre from top to tail
25g/1oz butter
30g/1oz sugar
50ml/2fl oz red wine vinegar
600ml/1pt beef stock
300ml/10fl oz red wine
1 sprig thyme
2 garlic cloves
15g/½oz flour

Cut the onion slices into half rings and fry them off in a pan into which 25g (1oz) of butter has been melted. When soft, add the sugar and red wine vinegar, and slowly simmer, stirring occasionally. When all the liquid has nearly gone, place in a container to cool. In a pan, put the beef stock and red wine and bring to the boil. Add the sprig of thyme and the garlic cloves and reduce the mixture by approximately three-quarters. Thicken by carefully adding and stirring in the flour. Include the red onion mix to this sauce and that's the gravy done.

Make the mashed potatoes by boiling in water until soft. Drain and mash before adding butter, the grated nutmeg and seasoning to taste. Boil the carrot triangles, together with the half orange, seasoning and butter until cooked.

Slightly brown the sausages in a hot pan, sprinkle with salt and pepper and place in the oven for about 10 minutes.

Dave Waller's Award-Winning Sausages with Creamed Potatoes.

North of England Pie and Cumin Seed Mushy Peas

Pie and Peas has long been a traditional Northern pub meal. Normally consisting of a pork pie and alarmingly unnaturally green peas, this recipe modernizes both the pie and the peas.

To make the pie
4 sheets filo pastry
1 onion, finely chopped
3 potatoes, peeled, chopped
300g/10½oz minced beef
400g/14oz can plum tomatoes
15ml/½fl oz milk
15ml/½fl oz water
1 tablespoon cornflour
½ teaspoon dried oregano
freshly ground pepper
1 tablespoon fresh mint, chopped
olive oil

Grease four 9cm pie dishes and, working with one filo sheet at a time, fold each in half and line the base and sides of the pan, before brushing the pastry lightly with oil. Line the base with baking paper and blind bake at 220°C (430°F) for 15 minutes or until golden. Meanwhile, cook the onion in an oiled pan over a medium-high heat until soft. Add the mince and cook until browned. Stir in the tomatoes and squash them with the back of a spoon. Combine cornflour, oregano and water. Stir through the mince and reduce the heat until the meat mix is simmering and cook for a further 5 minutes before seasoning with the pepper. Boil the potatoes until tender, drain, add the milk and mash. Stir in the chopped mint.

Remove pie cases from pans. Fill with mince, and top with potato. Season with more pepper if necessary and top with cumin seed peas.

For the cumin seed peas
450g frozen peas
125ml/4fl oz water
1 teaspoon cumin seeds
2 teaspoons butter
salt and black pepper

Warm the butter in a pan. Add the cumin and let it it sizzle before adding the frozen peas and pouring in the water. Let the mixture come to the boil. Add salt and pepper, and then boil for a further 3 minutes. Serve hot as an accompaniment to the pies, or, in keeping with northern tradition, just make the peas and enjoy as a snack!

Traditional Pie and Mushy Peas.

Hot-Pot Sausages with Creamy Mash and Rosemary Gravy

At the Whitehall Hotel near Blackburn, head chef Steve Waters has a variation on the theme of 'hot-pot'. To get the right meat texture, Steve suggests that you ask your butcher for equal quantities of shoulder and belly. Whilst you are at the butchers, ask him nicely for a few natural sausage skins!

1.5kg/3⅓lb minced lamb
3 carrots, peeled and coarsely chopped
1 large onion, peeled and coarsely chopped
3 'dry' potatoes (Steve suggests 'Maris Piper')
natural sausage skins
oil or butter to sauté
salt and pepper
red wine
veal stock concentrate (or ordinary stock)
chopped rosemary

Hot-Pot Sausages with Creamy Mash.

Sauté the onion, potatoes and carrots in a heavy-bottomed pan containing oil or butter. Mix well with the minced lamb, adding the salt and pepper.

If you have no sausage machine, stuff the mixture into the sausage skins by using a piping bag equipped with a large nozzle. Twist the ends and leave the sausages overnight (otherwise the skins will split when cooking). Fry in oil for about 2–3 minutes and then transfer the sausages to an oven pre-heated to 200°C (390°F) for a further 5–10 minutes.

Prepare a creamy potato mash in the normal way and, for the rosemary gravy, pour a glug of red wine into a pan, add in a pinch of chopped rosemary and reduce by half before adding roughly 500ml (16fl oz) of cold water to the pan. Heat, using the veal base concentrate or stock to thicken.

Braised Snowdonian Mutton Stew with Leek and Rosemary Cobbles

In September 2008, we were intending to visit the Laguna restaurant and bar, which forms part of the Park Plaza Hotel in Greyfriars Road, Cardiff. Floods in Monmouthshire (where we had other places to visit) impeded our travelling and we, unfortunately, returned home without actually getting to our destination. Despite that, Mark Freeman, head chef, at the Park Plaza, was kind enough to send us the recipes he intended us to photograph and which we are delighted to include here. The Laguna's menu offers a mix of the finest and freshest ingredients from Welsh suppliers, hence the fact that Snowdonian-reared and produced meat appears in this particular recipe.

Serves six

For the stew
1kg/2¼lb diced leg of Snowdonian mutton (lamb can be used)
2 celery stalks, roughly chopped
3 carrots, ditto
½ swede, cut into 12 same-sized chunks
6 shallots, peeled
6 small turnips, scrubbed and halved
10 whole black peppercorns
pinch of salt
1 sprig rosemary
1 sprig thyme
1ltr/2pt lamb stock (make from two good quality stock cubes)

For the cobbler top
350g/12oz self-raising flour
100g/3½oz unsalted butter
100g/3½oz finely chopped leek, lightly sautéed
10g/½oz parsley, finely chopped
10g/½oz rosemary, finely chopped
30ml/1fl oz plain natural yoghurt (mixed with 70ml cold water)

Place the mutton in a large casserole dish, together with the stock, vegetables, herbs, and peppercorns and season with salt. Bring to the boil and simmer gently for 1 hour.

Make the cobblers by rubbing together the butter and flour. Stir in the leeks and herbs and add enough of the yoghurt and water mix to make a soft, pliable dough. Roll the dough until it is about 2.5cm (1in) thick and then cut into 12 rounds. Place on top of the mutton stew, before baking at 200°C (390°F) for about 25–30 minutes, or until the cobblers are golden-brown. Serve immediately.

Pan-fried Cotswold Minute Steak with Creamed Potatoes, Celeriac and Rocket

Another well-loved recipe from the Cottage in the Wood, Malvern Wells, Worcestershire, using all locally supplied produce.

4 × 225g/8oz steaks
200g/7oz potato, diced
300g/10½oz celeriac, diced
200ml/7fl oz cream
1 teaspoon Dijon mustard
rocket salad
olive oil
seasoning

Cook the potatoes and celeriac together in a pan of boiling water for 4 minutes; drain and place in a hot oiled frying pan and fry for 1 minute. Add the cream and mustard and simmer until the cream has reduced slightly.

Prepare the rocket salad by drizzling with olive oil, adding a pinch of salt and turning carefully so that each leaf is coated with oil.

When all is ready to serve, have ready a hot griddle pan (slightly oiled). Season the steaks and fry for 30 seconds on each side. Serve immediately.

Pan-fried Cotswold Minute Steak with Creamed Potatoes.

Honey-Glazed Duck Breast, Tartlet of Confit Duck Leg, Roasted Butternut Squash Mash, Whimberry and Sloe Gin Sauce

Jonathan Waters, head chef at Whites at the Clockhouse, Tenbury Wells, Worcestershire, sources all the ingredients for his recipes locally and takes advantage of any situation in which he finds himself; 'if, for example, I get an unexpected bonus of partridge, I would take something else off the menu in order to make best use of the partridge. The whimberries in this recipe came from our wholesaler at Ludlow who got them from a local man who picks them in the wild.'

In other parts of the British Isles, whimberries are called whinberries. In the west they are known as whortleberries and elsewhere, Yorkshire, for instance, as bilberries. In Scotland they are called blaeberries.

4 duck breasts
honey to glaze breasts
black pepper

Remove any sinew, bone and excess fat; score the fat with a sharp knife. Take a thick-based cast-iron pan and place over a high heat. When the pan is smoking, place the duck breasts in skin side down. Keep draining the fat off as the breasts cook and adjust the heat. When the skin is golden and crispy, turn the breast over and cook for a further 10 minutes until the breast feels firm (the flesh should still be soft and pink in the middle). Remove the breasts from the heat and place on a tray; season the crispy fat with honey and black pepper.

For the tartlet filling
1 x 175g/6oz duck leg
600ml/1pt duck or goose fat
1 sprig fresh thyme
1 bunch fresh parsley
sea salt and black pepper

The night before, lightly salt the trimmed duck leg and leave in the fridge. The next day, wash the leg under cold running water to remove the salt and place in a small roasting tray with the fresh thyme and ground black pepper. Cover with the goose fat and then with foil before cooking in a low oven (150°C/300°F) for 1½–2 hours or until the meat starts to fall away from the bone. When cool, remove the meat from the bone and shred with a fork. Add chopped parsley and season with black pepper.

For the tartlet case
115g/4oz plain flour
75g/3oz butter
1 egg yolk
cold water
salt and pepper

Sieve the flour into a bowl with the salt and pepper. Dice the butter and rub it into the flour until it resembles breadcrumbs. Add the egg yolk and sufficient water to form pastry. Rest the pastry in the fridge for about 10 minutes. Roll out the pastry 0.5cm thick and cut out four 7cm circles. Place into pre-greased tart cases and lightly prick the bottoms with a fork Rest in the fridge for a further 10 minutes. Bake the cases in a pre-heated oven at 180°C (355°F) for 15–20 minutes or until light golden.

For the roasted butternut squash mash
225g/8oz butternut squash, peeled, de-seeded and chopped
60ml/2fl oz olive oil
sea salt and black pepper

Place the squash on a baking tray with the olive oil and seasoning. Roast in the oven 180°C (355°F) for 10–15 minutes until soft. Cool slightly, place in a food processor and process until smooth.

Assemble the tart by placing the seasoned and shredded duck confit into the pastry cases. Top with the butternut squash mash piped through a plain nozzle.

For the Whimberry and Sloe Gin Sauce
1 shallot, peeled and diced
60ml/2fl oz olive oil
300ml/10fl oz red wine
600ml/1pt chicken stock
1 dessertspoon tomato purèe
175g/6oz fresh whimberries
75ml/2½fl oz sloe gin
1 tablespoon redcurrant jelly
sea salt and black pepper

Soften the shallot on a medium heat with the olive oil. Add the red wine and reduce by half. Add the chicken stock, tomato purée, redcurrant jelly and 115g (4oz) of the whimberries. Reduce by half before removing from the heat, cooling a little and placing in a liquidizer. Process until smooth and pass through a sieve. Return to a clean pan and onto the heat and simmer (approx. 5 minutes). Add the sloe gin and remaining whimberries and seasoning.

Honey-Glazed Duck Breast and Tartlet of Confit Duck Leg.

Harome Chicken in Three Styles.

Harome Chicken in Three Styles – Roast Breast, Confit Leg, Chicken & Mushroom Pie

Devised by Robert Craggs at The Cadeby Inn, near Doncaster, South Yorkshire, Robert believes that the secret with imaginative regional cooking is to 'take something that everyone knows and to modernize it without spoiling the original.' Imagination is definitely the key – as Robert says, 'cooking is like a seed; nurture it and it will germinate and grow.'

Serves two
1 maize-fed chicken; whole
300ml/10fl oz duck fat
200g/7oz puff pastry sheet cut in four 10cm circles
200g/7oz wilted spinach
2 fondant potatoes
2 sprigs thyme
200g/7oz sautéed wild mushrooms
salt and pepper
chicken gravy
shiso cress
water
butter
1 egg yolk

Heat oven to 180°C (355°F). Remove the legs and breasts from the carcass. Place the legs and thighs into a saucepan, cover with duck fat and cook until tender. When tender, remove the thigh and trim the drumstick, then set aside. With the thigh meat, shred and roll into a ball with half of the sautéed mushrooms and season lightly with the salt and pepper.

Egg wash one of the pastry discs. Place the thigh meat ball on top before covering with remaining disc. Form a pie then egg wash. Bake in the oven until golden, approx. 10–15 minutes.

In a frying pan seal the chicken breast until golden on the skin, add a knob of butter and 100ml (3½fl oz) water into the pan. Place into the oven to cook for approx 12–15 minutes.

To serve, sauté the spinach and place into two small piles on the plate. On top, add the roast breast on one, and the pie on the other. In the middle, add the fondant potato and the trimmed drumstick at the end, as in image.

Decorate with thyme, sautéed mushrooms and chicken gravy before sprinkling the cress over to serve.

Pan-Fried Chicken Breasts in Bacon

Although it is obviously possible to use the cheaper, mass-produced chicken breasts currently available, if finances allow and a local producer can be sourced, use free-range chicken breasts for this recipe – the overall flavour of the dish will be greatly enhanced.

4 chicken breasts
4 slices bacon
1 small tub soft herb and garlic cheese
60g/2oz butter (or a good 'glug' of olive oil)

Gently flatten each chicken breast with the palm of your hand and make a pocket in each one with a sharp knife. Place a good teaspoon of herb and garlic cheese in the pocket created and wrap a rasher of bacon, spiral-fashion, around the breast, securing it if necessary with a wooden cocktail stick.

Put the butter or oil in a large heavy-bottomed frying pan and bring up to heat, taking care if using butter that it doesn't burn. Gently fry the chicken breasts, turning frequently, and occasionally inserting the point of the knife to check on cooking progress in the thickest part of the meat.

A Plate of Harome-Reared 'Loose Birds' Duck with Garden Lemon Thyme Mash, Traditional Yorkshire Sauce

Robert Cragg's recipe for *Harome Chicken in Three Styles* uses chicken sourced from a village in North Yorkshire which is also home to Andrew and Jacquie Pern at the Star Inn, Harome, Helmsley. Very kindly (especially as Andrew has produced a recipe book of his own, *Black Pudding and Foie Gras*; May 2008), he submitted the following:

A complete surprise for the guests – when this appears in front of them rather than the normal 'pub fayre' of a crispy, leathery well-done duck axed in half straight through the middle. The Star Inn turns out a plate of six separate components, all coming from Paul Talling's ducks, reared just outside the village – all that is except the *foie gras*, which comes from further afield, and some of the eggs from Sim and Josie Barker's farm around the corner from the pub (down past the duck pond, funnily enough). The sauce, a traditional classic, can be found in the *Repertoire de la Cuisine*: a little book of biblical qualities for any chef [Author's Note: *A reference work on French cuisine with French text. This book is a world renowned classic and is a basic reference to the cuisine of Escoffier – with an alphabetical listing of French terms, and 6,000 dishes for hors-d'oeuvre, soups, eggs and fish, entrees, salads, pastas, vegetables, pastries*]. The orange and port-based sauce is a perfect partner to the rich, fatty duck. In fact, *Duck à l'Orange* all over again!

4 duck legs
2 duck breasts
4 duck eggs
300g/10½oz duck *foie gras*
4 duck chipolatas
10g/½oz lemon thyme
1 orange
1 bay leaf
1 star anise
1ltr/2pt duck fat
200ml/7fl oz red wine
100g/3½oz redcurrant jelly
150g/5oz sugar
500g/1lb mashed potato
100g/3½oz butter
100ml/3½fl oz cream
a little white wine vinegar
100ml/3½fl oz duck 'jus'
seasoning

Confit the duck legs in the duck fat with the star anise and bay leaf in an oven for 2½ hours at 140°C (285°F). Peel the orange and cut the peel into julienne strips (removing all the white). Place in a pan with the red wine, sugar and redcurrant jelly. Juice the left-over orange and add to the pan as well. Reduce until it becomes syrup, and add the duck 'jus'. Once the duck legs have cooled down, split the thigh and the drumstick before plac-ing onto a baking tray. Boil the potatoes, drain and mash. Reduce the butter and cream by half and add to the mash. Season to taste. Add the lemon thyme leaves and keep warm. Grill the chipolatas until just cooked and put on the baking tray with the leg and thigh. Pan-fry the duck breasts until the skin is crispy but still there. Place on the tray and then in a pre-heated oven at 190°C (375°F) for 5 minutes.

Meanwhile, reheat the mash and put into a piping bag, poach the duck eggs in simmer-ing water with a little white wine vinegar for about 3 minutes, keep warm. Pan-fry the *foie gras* until it becomes spongy. Pipe five turrets of mash around the outside of the plate and one in the centre. Place each ingredient on one of the mashed potato turrets, slice and save the duck breast for the centre of the plate, drizzle sauce around and over the dish ingredients. Serve immediately.

Harome-Reared Duck with Lemon Thyme Mash. (Photo: Andrew and Jacquie Pern at The Star Inn)

GOOSNARGH DUCKS

Goosnargh (pronounced Goosner) is a village near Preston, Lancashire. One could be forgiven for thinking that the village should be more famous for geese rather than ducks, but most historians think that the name refers to a Saxon chieftain. The Goosnargh duck is a white-feathered, yellow-beaked cross between an Aylesbury and a Peking. 'They're majestic creatures, very content and very easy to rear,' says duck breeder Reg Johnson, whose ducks are kept not on a pond but in a large barn, with troughs and nipple feeders so that they can drink and get their heads wet. It is an old wives' tale that ducks need to swim to live and Johnson says that if he let the ducks onto water they would become diseased. These particular 'Goosnarghs' are killed at 56 days old and hung for up to 48 hours, which increases the meat's flavour.

Goosnargh village.

'Boar's Nest' Goosnargh Corn-Fed Duck Breast. (Photo: Simon Rogers and Dina Hanchett at The Boar's Nest)

'Boar's Nest' Goosnargh Corn-Fed Duck Breast; Bubble and Squeak in a Lattice Puff

Simon Rogers and Dina Hanchett of the Boar's Nest, Kingston-upon-Hull, East Yorkshire are just two of the many restaurateurs who prefer to use local produce and in particular, source their meat from places with a proven history of supplying good quality ingredients. You cannot, apparently, get a better duck than a 'Goosnargh' duck!

Serves one
1 Goosnargh corn-fed duck breast
75g/3oz 'floury' mashed potato
75g/3oz cooked vegetables (cabbage, carrot and spinach)
100g/3½oz puff pastry
50ml/2fl oz port
150ml/5fl oz chicken stock
10g/½oz butter
salt and pepper
egg wash
oil

Remove the fat from the back of the breast and season both sides with salt and pepper before sealing the breast in hot oil for 30 seconds on each side. Remove from the pan and allow to cool. Roughly chop the vegetables and mix them together in a bowl with the mashed potato. Season; form in 'duck breast' shape and place on top of the previously sealed breast.

Roll out the puff pastry until it is approximately 0.5cm thick and slightly larger than the breast. Gently roll a lattice cutter across the pastry; open the cut pastry and wrap it over the breast, tucking any excess underneath. Egg wash and place on a lightly oiled tray before baking in a medium oven (180–200°C/355–390°F) for 12 minutes.

For the sauce, mix together the stock and the port, heating gently until the mixture has reduced by three-quarters. Remove from the heat before stirring in the butter. Position the duck breast in the centre of a warmed plate and, finally, drizzle the sauce around.

Pan-Roasted Tidenham Chase Duck Breast; Herb-Crushed Purple Truffle Potatoes with a Medley of Feves, Mange-Tout and Baby Carrots, set in a Bramble and Merlot Jus

This recipe, from the menu at The Bell, Skenfrith, Monmouthshire, uses locally sourced duck combined with vegetables and fruit from their own organic kitchen garden. The Bell was reopened by Janet and William Hutchings in 2001 and they are part way through conversion to organic/biodynamic status in the garden, which, as Janet says, 'just means you have to be one step ahead of the bug and insect life!' They now supply all their own salad crops, feves, chard and baby vegetables, as well as herbs and some soft fruits. Both Janet and William are very conscious of 'food miles' and source all other produce from as close to The Bell as possible. They are also members of the 'slow food movement'.

Take four trimmed duck breasts and cook them (skin side down first) in a dry frying pan – they will exude enough fat to save them from sticking. Test with knife when cooked; ideally they should be pink inside. Leave to rest.

Prepare the *Feves, Mange-tout and Baby Carrots* and cook *al dente*: toss in a small amount of butter and season.

Cook and roughly crush the *Purple Truffle Potatoes* (bought from your local producer or, better still, grown in your own garden) and mix in chopped garden herbs, together with a knob of butter.

Make a *Bramble and Merlot Jus* by using the juices from the duck: thicken and make a sauce with some of the vegetable water, a 'glug' of merlot and poached blackberries.

To serve, use a large round pastry cutter and place in middle of plate, fill with crushed potatoes. Slice the duck breast at an angle and place in a circular fashion on top of the potato. Arrange the garden vegetables around the plate and drizzle over the *jus* (arranging the blackberries around the plate). Enjoy!

The kitchen garden at The Bell, Skenfrith, Monmouthshire.

The Bell at Skenfrith. (Photo: Janet and William Hutchings)

Scottish Venison with Fresh Pear Chutney

This is a recipe from the wonderfully successful 'Game's On' campaign, which, along with 'Game-to-Eat', aims to support and promote the supply of local, healthy seasonal food and increase the amount of game sold through supermarkets.

900g/2lb venison fillet or boned leg
1 teaspoon thyme
1 bay leaf
olive oil
salt and pepper

Roll and tie the meat with butcher's string. Mix together the herbs and pepper and rub into the meat. In a flameproof casserole, heat the olive oil and seal the meat on all sides before seasoning with salt and roasting at 180°C (355°F) for 20 minutes.

For the fresh pear chutney
2 pears, peeled, cored and roughly chopped
1 small chilli, de-seeded and finely chopped
1 garlic clove, crushed
1 small piece ginger, grated
1 cinnamon stick
55g (2oz) sugar
2 tablespoons apple cider vinegar
pinch of ground cloves

Place all the chutney ingredients into a small heavy-bottomed pan and cook gently until the sugar has dissolved. Simmer for a further 10–15 minutes, or until the pears are soft.

GROATY DICK

Groaty Dick or Groaty Pudding is a very substantial casserole, made from shin of beef, onions, leeks and groats – oats before the husk has been hulled. In poor families any cheaper cuts of meat or even pieces of bacon from the family pig would have gone into the dish and it was intended that it just simmered and cooked on the kitchen grate whilst the Midlands men-folk were out doing what ever Midland men-folk did in the way of work. After they had eaten Groaty Dick, they may well have finished of with a piece of Filbelly – the local name for bread pudding.

Scottish Venison with Fresh Pear Chutney.

Parcelled Exmoor Venison Steaks

There are many things one can do with all cuts of venison, the shin, for instance, sliced into small pieces, can be treated exactly as a shin of veal; stews and casseroles can be made from cuts that traditionally require long, slow cooking and the meat can also be easily adapted for established recipes such as suet puddings. Roasting can, however, sometimes lead to disappointment, due to the fact that venison is such a lean meat. Judging the cooking time for a joint of venison largely depends on the particular joint and, to some extent, what type of deer the meat comes from. Red and fallow can be very rare in the manner of roast beef, but roe should possibly be cooked a little more like lamb. Of course there is no reason why any joint shouldn't be 'well done' if that's how you prefer it.

4 loin or haunch steaks; cut about 1–2cm (½–¾in) thick
30g/1oz butter
1 medium onion, skinned and finely chopped
225g/8oz mushrooms, wiped and sliced
115ml/4fl oz red wine
115ml/4fl oz soured cream or yoghurt
2 tablespoons lemon juice
seasoning

Marinade the steaks for 24 hours. There is no exact science to preparing a marinade and a typical one that will work well with heavier meats such as venison is likely to combine some or all of the following ingredients: a bottle of red wine (full-bodied rather than the lighter Gamay grape type), two tablespoons of red wine vinegar (or rather less of balsamic), chopped onion and garlic, herbs, a pinch of mixed dried spices and the same of grated nutmeg, a bay leaf or two, a couple of glugs of olive oil and, if you can get them, half a dozen juniper berries.

Melt the butter in a large frying pan and seal the venison steaks well, keeping them flat by pressing firmly down with the blade of the spatula. Remove from the pan and place each on individual squares of foil cut about 20cm square.

Add the onions and mushrooms to the butter remaining in the pan and cook for 5 minutes. Stir in the red wine and the lemon juice and bring to the boil. Reduce the liquid by half, then remove from the heat and stir in the soured cream or yoghurt. Season well.

Place a quarter of the mushroom mixture on top of each steak, then shape the foil into parcels, sealing well. Put the parcels into a shallow ovenproof dish and bake in the oven at 180°C (355°F) for 30–40 minutes, until the steaks are tender. To serve, place each parcel on a plate and take sealed to the table, allowing your guests to open their own. Accompany with small new potatoes, boiled in their jackets and sautéed in butter, together with green beans.

Slow-Roast Pork Belly with Chorizo Mash

Vernon Blackmore of The Anchor Inn, Woodbridge, Suffolk is an enthusiastic chef and, as with most who love to give long-established regional country recipes that little extra 'lift' and 'twist', he insists on using local produce whenever possible.

1kg/2¼lb belly pork (skin on)
1kg/2¼lb main crop potato
200g/7oz cooking chorizo
2 cloves garlic (finely diced)
seasonal vegetables
250ml/8fl oz vegetable oil
4 tablespoons olive oil
250ml/8fl oz red wine
350ml/12⅓fl oz water
1 teaspoon flour
salt and pepper
fresh rosemary sprigs

Slow-Roast Pork Belly with Chorizo Mash.

Sprinkle a generous amount of salt and pepper on to the bottom of a roasting tray before adding a few sprigs of rosemary and the olive oil. Place the pork belly on top and put into the hottest part of a pre-heated oven set at 220°C (430°F). After 20 minutes, turn the temperature down to 180°C (355°F) and add the water into the tray. Cook for 1 hour and then pour in the wine. Cook for a further 45 minutes. Have a separate pan of water boiling ready for the vegetables.

Meanwhile, prepare the chorizo mash. Peel then cut the potatoes into equal sized pieces and place in cold salted water. Bring to the boil and simmer for approximately 20 minutes. Check they are ready with a sharp knife, drain and leave to stand for 10 minutes. Make the chorizo oil whilst the potatoes are standing. Peel the skin from the chorizo and cut into small pieces. Heat the vegetable oil on a medium heat, add in the chorizo and simmer until the chorizo turns a dark brown. Remove the pan from the heat and add the finely diced garlic. Mash the potatoes and pour in the chorizo oil. Mix well and season to taste. Keep this warm.

Remove the pork belly from the oven, take it out of the tray and leave it to rest for 10 minutes in a warm place. Skim the fat from the remaining juices in the tray, then place the roasting tray onto a low heat and bring to the boil. Sprinkle in a teaspoon of flour. Stir vigorously until it thickens. Season to taste and use this as gravy. Place the vegetables into the boiling water, blanch and prepare for serving. Carve the belly pork into four pieces, place a large spoonful of chorizo mash in the centre of the plate, and place the vegetables to the side and the belly pork on top of the mash. Pour over the gravy and serve.

NB: Vernon offers the following tip: to save a last-minute panic, the mash and the vegetables can be prepared ahead of time and then reheated just prior to serving.

Aberdeen Beef Caesar Salad

Fiona Seddon is a crofter and also runs a self-catering enterprise in the Highlands. She breeds Aberdeen Angus and uses their steak to make this Caesar salad with a difference. She does, however, admit that it tastes equally as good with meat from other locally produced beef and says that the recipe 'works well with leftover cooked roast beef too.'

450g/1lb lean Aberdeen Angus rump or sirloin steak
1 tablespoon freshly chopped chives
salt and pepper
3 tablespoons olive oil
1 large Cos lettuce
75g/3oz prepared bread croutons

For the dressing
10ml/⅓fl oz Dijon mustard
30ml/1fl oz lemon juice
60ml/2fl oz extra-virgin olive oil
2 tablespoons freshly grated Parmesan
5ml/¼fl oz anchovy sauce

In a small bowl, mix together the chives, seasoning and olive oil. Use to brush the streaks on both sides and then set to one side for 5 minutes. Cook the steak under a pre-heated grill or on the barbeque (rare: 2½ minutes on each side; medium: 4 minutes; well done: 6 minutes on each side – based on a 2cm (¾in) thick steak). Transfer to a plate and leave to rest for 5 minutes. Slice on the diagonal and place in a large salad bowl. Add the lettuce leaves and the croutons.

Prepare the dressing by putting all the ingredients into a screw-topped jar and shaking well before drizzling over the salad and garnishing with a little extra Parmesan. Serve immediately.

PARSLEY AND 'LICKY' PIES

You might suppose that, as the term 'squab' is used to describe a young pigeon, a Squab Pie would contain pigeon meat – well, not in Devon it doesn't, and if you find it on a pub menu in or around the South Molton area, don't be surprised to find that the meat element is made up of tender lamb combined with apples and onions! Choose a Parsley Pie, however, and you are on much safer ground: you're likely to be served a quiche-like affair where a couple of handfuls of chopped-up parsley have been laid in a pastry base and covered with eggs and cream before being oven baked. Cold, it can be cut into slices and taken on a picnic. Another local favourite that can be eaten either hot or cold is the dubious sounding 'Licky Pie'. To make it, line a dish with pastry, boil some leeks and cut them into small pieces before placing them in the pie base together with bacon, egg, cream, salt and pepper. Cover the whole lot with a pastry 'lid' and bake until the top is golden-brown.

Hand Raised Grouse and Foie Gras Pie
with Apricot and Wild Mushrooms

It seems that in years gone by, many regions had their own pie particular to the locality. Of course the most famous of these must be the Leicestershire Melton Mowbray pork pie, but others included the 'squab' pies of Devon – not, as one might suppose, made of young pigeon, but of mutton and apple; the Shropshire pie containing rabbit meat, and the Coventry pie, which unlike its Devon counterpart, did actually consist of pigeons. Almost any meat can be included in a game pie, but the most commonly used is that of pheasant, partridge, pigeon, wild duck, venison, rabbit and hare. It is a good way of using older birds, leaving young ones for roasting and stir-fries.

Martyn Nail, the Executive Chef of Claridges Hotel, Mayfair, kindly agreed to share this recipe. He says:

The hand raised pie is a British classic, which done well is still very much enjoyed today. It is a feature on the winter menus when the game items are in season. Guests like to come down to the kitchen and see it prepared, as it always draws interest. This wonderfully crafted pie is so scarcely seen and understood these days.

To make the hot water pastry:
300ml/10fl oz milk
300ml/10fl oz water
350g/12oz lard
1.35kg/3lb plain flour
2 teaspoons salt
egg wash – 2 egg yolks with equal amount of cold water

For the filling
5 grouse, bones removed and flesh checked for shot
1 'lobe' duck foie gras
200g/7oz mixed wild mushrooms
15 dried apricots
8 leaves gelatine
30ml/1fl oz ruby port
15ml/½fl oz Madeira
salt
white pepper
2 sprigs thyme

For lining the pie
500g/1lb streaky bacon

Consommé jelly
500ml/16fl oz chicken consommé
10 leaves gelatine

Heat the water, milk and lard to 85°C (185°F). Put the flour and the salt on to a bench and form a 'well' in the centre. Gradually add the liquid to the flour, stirring as you do so. Work the ingredients lightly to form the pastry. Wrap in cling film and chill. Allow the pastry to come to room temperature then roll out to 0.5cm (¼in). Cut the pastry to the shape that best fits and lines your chosen mould (remembering to reserve some pastry in order to form the pie lid).

Line the greased mould with pastry, making sure to overlap the edges and press it tightly into the tin, leaving a 3cm (1¼in) border of pastry protruding over the edge of the tin. Line the pastry with streaky bacon.

Place all the ingredients for the filling in a bowl and mix in the seasoning. Allow to stand for 1 hour before arranging the filling in the pie, forming a mosaic pattern. Close over the bacon and bring up the overlapping pastry. Now prepare your lid and make one or two steam holes, brush the pastry with an egg wash and decorate. Brush the top of the overlap with the egg wash and apply the lid to the pie. Allow to rest for at least 30 minutes before cooking.

Cook at 200°C (390°F) until golden (approx 15 minutes), then cover with foil and cook until you get a core temperature of 54°C (130°F). Allow to rest at room temperature for 25–30 minutes and then cool in a fridge for 1 hour or until the pastry sets.

Soften the gelatine in cold water and bring the consommé to the boil. Add the gelatine and allow to cool. Then pour the prepared jelly through the steam hole: allow this to set in the fridge for 20 minutes before toping up with the jelly again. Repeat this process until the jelly reaches the top of the steam hole. Allow to stand for at least 24 hours before removing the pie from the mould and slicing.

PREPARING MEAT FOR A GAME PIE

To prepare the meat it can be cubed and marinated prior to being browned off in oil in a heavy-bottomed frying pan or even simply cut and browned in order to seal the meat. Alternatively, place bird carcasses in a large pan together with seasoning and a bouquet garni before covering with stock or water and simmering with the lid on until the meat begins to part from the bone and can be cut away in good-sized pieces. After taking off the best pieces, break up the remains of the carcass and return to the pot. Continue simmering to create a thick stock for later use. If the pie you are making is intended to be eaten cold, one way of ensuring that the filling sets after cooking is to include a pig's trotter in with the stock ingredients.

Rump of Spring Denby Dale Lamb, Fondant Potato, Cabbage, Rosemary Jus

The easy availability of quality meat in Yorkshire inspired James Brown of The Ivy, The Grange Hotel, Clifton, York, to develop a classic dish into something special. Buying locally is important: 'Food is fresher and it helps the local economy and I have found that once you establish a good rapport with a supplier and/or producer, they will always give preference to regular customers.' In James' opinion (and in common with that of several other chefs with whom we spoke), meat has to be hung to bring out the best flavours: 'A rib-eye, for instance, hung for twenty-eight days is better than one hung for only a week.'

Rump of Spring Denby Dale Lamb.

4 jacket potatoes
4 rumps spring lamb
6 sprigs rosemary
1 block butter
2 cloves garlic
1 Savoy cabbage
1 carrot
½ a celeriac
4 rashers smoked streaky bacon
1 tablespoon duck fat
150ml/5fl oz double cream
2ltr/3½pt good chicken stock
3 shallots
¼pt Madeira
oil
seasoning

Slice the long edges off the potato. Cut with a metal ring and trim the edges. Melt the butter in a heavy-bottomed pan before adding the garlic and a sprig of rosemary. Arrange the potatoes in the pan so they are not on top of each other. Cook over a low heat, turning occasionally until golden-brown and soft in the middle.

Slice the shallots, put into a pan with the rosemary and the Madeira and slowly reduce. When the Madeira is reduced, add the chicken stock and start to reduce to the required consistency – the exact thickness of which will depend on the individual's personal preference.

Cut the carrots and celeriac into battens approximately 0.5cm square and 2.5cm long. Slice the cabbage very thin, discarding the thick stalk. Cut the bacon into lardoons and heat the duck fat in a pan. When hot, add the bacon and cook until lightly coloured. Add the carrot and celeriac and fry for 4 minutes. Add the cabbage and cook for a further 4 minutes until *al dente*. Remove from the heat and spread the cabbage mix on a tray and put in the fridge to cool.

Heat a little oil in a frying pan, season the lamb and seal it all over. Place on a tray, skin side down, and cook in a pre-heated oven at 180°C (355°F) for 7 minutes. Once cooked, remove from the oven and place it to one side in order to rest. While the lamb is resting, reduce the cream by half and warm the potato fondant in the oven. Add the cabbage to the cream and season. Serve just as soon as hot.

Rabbit Curry with Ginger

Very definitely a modern mixture of traditional British country cooking and an Eastern influence of curry and ginger!

Serves six
750g/1²/₃lb rabbit meat, cubed
60g/2oz butter
2 tablespoons sunflower oil
salt and pepper
300ml/10fl oz game or chicken stock
2 tablespoons flour
2 tablespoons curry powder
½ teaspoon turmeric
pinch of ground cardamon
3cm (1¼in) piece of peeled and grated ginger
2 shallots, finely chopped
3 tablespoons tomato purée
15g/½oz sultanas, soaked in hot water to cover

Heat half the butter and one teaspoon of oil in a frying pan and fry the shallots until they have softened and started to colour, then toss in the drained sultanas. Set aside and keep warm.

In a clean frying pan add the remaining butter and oil, and cook the rabbit pieces quickly until they are cooked through. Remove them with a slotted spoon and keep warm. Set aside. Pour off all but one tablespoon of the fat left in the frying pan. Add curry powder, spices, flour and tomato purée and cook for 2 minutes. Next, pour in the stock and stir vigorously, scraping up all the caramelized bits from the bottom of the pan. Bring the sauce to the boil, and cook for 10–15 minutes until the sauce starts to thicken – add more stock if it is too thick. Season with salt and pepper. Add the rabbit pieces to the sauce and cook for a few minutes, then serve with basmati rice.

The Clocktower Burger

Such is its reputation, during our trips around Yorkshire we were continually being asked if we were visiting Rudding Park, near Harrogate. Stephanie Moon, Executive Chef, told us of a simple but very special burger developed at their 'Clocktower' eatery.

600g/1⅓lb organic minced beef
1 teaspoon Lea and Perrin's sauce
2 shallots, peeled and finely chopped
4 mini gherkins (or ½ a large one), finely chopped
2 teaspoons capers
1 heaped tablespoon tomato ketchup
salt and pepper
vegetable oil for frying

The Clocktower Burger. (Photo: Stephanie Moon at The Clocktower, Rudding Park)

Place all of the ingredients above in a bowl and using a large spoon bring together. Season with a good pinch of salt and pepper. Using a ring mould, form the four burgers from the mixture (if you do not have a mould use a palette knife and shape the mixture into the classic burger style on a chopping board). Heat some vegetable oil in a frying pan. Place the burgers in the pan and cook on both sides for approximately 2 minutes each side over a moderate heat until golden-brown. Use the palette knife to flip the burgers over. Once brown on both sides, place in the oven at 180°C (355°F) for 6 minutes.

Stephanie says: 'These burgers are special because they do not shrink. Adrian hangs the beef well so the tenderness and flavour really shines through. There is no excess fat released during cooking, so what you see is what you get. This is a truly handsome burger!'

These burgers appear on the menu at the Clocktower accompanied by real chips, onion rings in Black Sheep beer batter, red onion marmalade and a side salad. The burger itself is topped with a couple of rashers of Wensleydale bacon, Wensleydale cheese and comes in a sesame bun made from Yorkshire milled flour. A real Yorkshire winner.

BEAN JAR

'Bean Jar' is a sort of *cassoulet* made with a pig's trotter or piece of beef, haricot beans, dried herbs, onions and carrots. The beans are soaked overnight and then both beans and meat would briefly be boiled before being transferred to an earthenware pot (the Bean Jar), covered with water and cooked in a slow oven for several hours. In days gone by, many Guernsey families would take their Bean Jar to the local bakers on a Saturday evening, placing their jars in the cooling ovens (as no bread was baked on the Sunday). In the morning the cooked meal was collected and the baker was paid per jar. The Bean Jar was then often stored and eaten on Monday, as the women were too busy washing cloths to cook, sometimes reheating the remainder on Tuesday because this was ironing day.

~ VEGETARIAN ~

Many people who have no intention of becoming totally committed vegetarians can still enjoy meals and recipes that do not rely on meat and fish. Undoubtedly, the realization is growing that for healthy hearts, slim figures, good digestion, nutritional balance, and economy, there are alternatives to simple omelettes or cauliflower cheese. What is more, with the increasing popularity of regionally produced cheeses, vegetables and fruit, fresh and interesting varieties are readily available. Fresh laid free-range eggs, colourful roots, crisp leafy greens, succulent pods and seeds are far too delicious and nutritious to be relegated to the supporting role in many recipes and they can offer an endless and tempting source of main meals.

Wensleydale Sauce Vegetable Moussaka

As with the recipe for *Rabbit Curry with Ginger* (*see* page 113), this recipe combines a traditional British cheese with foreign cooking methods and was adapted from a Greek recipe by one of the authors!

100g/3½oz lentils, soaked overnight and drained
450g/1lb tomatoes, skinned and chopped
450g/1lb potatoes, peeled and thinly sliced
1 large aubergine, thinly sliced
1 bay leaf
1 teaspoon dried oregano
1 teaspoon soft dark-brown sugar
salt and freshly ground black pepper
sunflower oil, for frying

For the Wensleydale Sauce
25g/1oz soft margarine
25g/1oz wholemeal flour
300ml/10fl oz milk
100g/3½oz Wensleydale cheese, grated
150ml/5fl oz plain, unsweetened yoghurt
1 egg
pinch of grated nutmeg

Cook the lentils in boiling, unsalted water for 1 hour and then drain. Simmer the tomatoes with the bay leaf, oregano, sugar, salt and pepper for 20 minutes before stirring the lentils into the tomato mixture and simmering for a further 10 minutes, stirring until it thickens. Heat the oil and fry the aubergine slices a few at a time over moderate heat until they begin to colour. Cook the potato slices in boiling salted water for 10 minutes or until they begin to soften. In a greased casserole dish, make layers of the tomato and lentil sauce, aubergines and potatoes (finishing with a layer of potatoes on top).

Melt the margarine and stir in the flour. Cook for 1 minute; remove the pan from the heat before beginning to gradually stirring in the milk and the yoghurt. Bring to the boil, and then simmer for 3 minutes. Remove from the heat. Beat in half the cheese and the egg and season with salt, pepper and nutmeg. Pour the sauce over the dish and sprinkle the remaining cheese on top. Stand the casserole on a baking sheet and cook in a pre-heated oven at 190°C (375°F) for 35–40 minutes, or until the sauce is bubbling and browned.

Glamorgan Sausages

Glamorgan sausages, despite their name, contain no meat but are made of cheese, breadcrumbs, herbs and chopped onions (or, for that truly authentic Welsh taste, leeks!).

Makes eight sausages
175g/6oz fresh breadcrumbs
100g/3½oz Caerphilly cheese, grated
1 onion, or a leek, finely chopped
1 tablespoon chopped fresh parsley
large pinch mustard powder
salt and pepper
2 eggs, separated
4 tablespoons fresh milk
15ml/½fl oz vegetable oil
15g/½oz butter
a little flour

In a large bowl, mix together the breadcrumbs, cheese, onion/leek, parsley and mustard. Season to taste. Add one whole egg and the yolk of the other before mixing once more. Add enough milk to ensure that the mixture is moist enough to bind together when cooking. Divide the mix into eight and roll them gently into sausage shapes.

Beat the remaining egg white on a plate until frothy and then dip the sausages into the egg white before rolling each one in flour to coat. Heat the oil and the butter in a frying pan and fry the sausages for between 5–10 minutes until golden-brown. They can be served cold, but traditionally, they are eaten hot with potatoes.

Beery Batter Yorkshire Puddings

Although traditionally served with roast beef, Yorkshire puddings can also be used as a base for many vegetarian dishes. The inclusion of a little Yorkshire Bitter makes them truly Yorkshire!

125g/4½oz sifted plain flour
pinch of sea salt
2 egg yolks and 1 egg white
300ml/10fl oz semi-skimmed milk
splash of Yorkshire Bitter
a little rapeseed oil

Beat the egg, beer and milk into the flour and salt until you have a smooth batter. Beat well and leave to stand. Pour a drop of rapeseed oil into each cup of a twelve-cup pudding tin (to make individual Yorkshires) or into the base of a roasting tin and pre-heat for 5 minutes in an oven set at 220°C (430°F). Pour the batter into a jug and then into the heated tin before baking at the same temperature for 15–20 minutes or until golden.

NB: Many Yorkshire pudding aficionados heat the oil in the cooking tray by leaving on a hot hob until the oil bubbles – the secret of a successful pudding is, they claim, having the oil hot enough to start with.

Chestnut and Cabbage Pudding

Carol Wilson, cookery writer and regular contributor to *Country Smallholding* magazine, suggests the following as a winter treat.

1 large cabbage
50g/2oz butter
25g/1oz flour
300ml/10fl oz vegetable stock
150–175g/5–6oz breadcrumbs
900g/2lb chestnuts, peeled and cooked
1 onion, chopped

Reserve a few large cabbage leaves and finely chop the rest. Heat half of the butter in a pan and stir in the flour. Cook for 1 minute over a low heat before adding the stock and stirring until smooth. Add the chopped cabbage leaves and onions and cook for a few minutes. Scald the whole cabbage leaves in boiling water and drain them well. Line a large buttered pudding basin with the breadcrumbs and then line with the cabbage leaves, so that part of the leaves stand above the rim (save some leaves to cover the top).

Fill with alternate layers of chestnuts (to save time cooking, use canned or vacuum-packed chestnuts) and cabbage. Melt the remaining butter and pour over the top layer. Cover with the remaining cabbage leaves. Cover with a lid or double thickness of pleated greaseproof paper, then with a double thickness of pleated foil – to allow for expansion as the pudding cooks. Tie securely and place in a large pan. Pour in boiling water to come halfway up the basin and steam for 1 hour. Turn out the pudding onto a serving plate and serve immediately.

Vegetarian Scotch Eggs

Ask many vegetarians what they miss most and Scotch eggs usually appear in their list. Terry Atkins, who supplies several vegetarian menus to tea-rooms and cafés in Somerset, makes his Scotch eggs the following way.

Makes four eggs
150g/5oz Sosmix
250ml/8fl oz cold water
4 eggs, hard-boiled and de-shelled
2 eggs, lightly beaten
200g/7oz breadcrumbs
125g/4½oz flour
1 teaspoon chopped chives
1 teaspoon tomato purée
1 teaspoon Marmite (love it or hate it – it's optional!)
salt and pepper
sunflower oil for frying

Place the Sosmix (vegetarian sausage mix) in a bowl and add the cold water before mixing together well (the mixture may look too runny at first). Add the chives, the purée and the Marmite, along with the salt and pepper seasoning and mix well. Place the mix in the fridge and chill for 20 minutes. Season the flour and roll the eggs in it. Place a small amount of the Sosmix in the palm of the hand and shape it around one of the eggs, filling in any gaps until a quarter of the Sosmix has been used. Repeat the procedure with the other three eggs. Dip the covered eggs thoroughly in the beaten eggs and roll in the breadcrumbs until completely covered. Chill for a further 10 minutes.

Heat the oil in a pan until it reaches optimum temperature (check by dropping in a small cube of bread – if the cube sizzles and quickly browns, the oil is ready). Cook the eggs, two at a time, for about 8 minutes or until crisp and golden.

Wild Mushroom and Garlic Tart

Cheat by making this tart from ready-made puff pastry.

Serves six
2 medium onions, quartered
30g/1oz butter
300g/10oz mixed wild mushrooms, thickly sliced
2 garlic cloves, crushed
home-made puff pastry or 375g/13¼oz packet puff pastry
3 tablespoons double cream
50g/2oz English Derby cheese
1 egg
salt and pepper
fresh thyme leaves, for garnish

Boil the onion quarters in salted water for about 5 minutes and drain thoroughly. Melt the butter in a frying pan and fry the onion pieces, mushroom and garlic over a high heat until all the liquid has gone. Season, stir in the cream and cook for about 1 minute before setting aside to cool.

Roll out the puff pastry on a cold floured board until it is quite thin. Place on a flat greased and floured tray and brush the pastry edge with beaten egg to create a 1cm (½in) border before spooning the mushroom mixture into the centre and topping with the cheese. Bake in the oven at 200°C (390°F) for about 25–30 minutes or until the pastry is golden-brown and puffed up. Serve hot, garnished with thyme leaves.

PEA SCADDING AND FRUTTERS

The origin of eating fried peas or *carlings* on the fifth Sunday in Lent or, as it is known in Bishop Auckland, *Carling Sunday*, seems to be wrapped in complete obscurity, but local tradition gives a possible origin to this old and still prevailing custom. In times gone by, a famine was raging in Newcastle and a ship foundered on the north-east coast, losing its cargo of peas. This was eventually washed up and greatly appreciated by the local communities and so the custom was perpetuated in commemoration of the event. Traditionally, the carlings are *scadded* or soaked overnight in water, boiled well and fried in butter before being served with vinegar and buttered bread.

Elsewhere, ever mindful of the paucities of Lent, a custom, used up ingredients in order to provide simple food, was the eating of currant fritters or 'frutters' on the Thursday following Ash Wednesday.

Mrs Beeton suggested the following recipe:

½pt of milk, 2 tablespoonfuls of flour, 4 eggs, 3 tablespoonfuls of boiled rice, 3 tablespoonfuls of currants, sugar to taste, a very little grated nutmeg, hot lard or clarified dripping.

Put the milk into a basin with the flour, which should previously be rubbed to a smooth batter with a little cold milk; stir these ingredients together; add the well-whisked eggs, the rice, currants, sugar, and nutmeg. Beat the mixture for a few minutes, and, if not sufficiently thick, add a little more boiled rice; drop it, in small quantities, into a pan of boiling lard or clarified dripping; fry the fritters a nice brown and, when done, drain them on a piece of blotting-paper, before the fire. Pile them on a white d'oyley, strew over sifted sugar, and serve them very hot. Send a cut lemon to table with them.

The Pudding

It's a funny thing the way the fortunes of the classic British puddings go. In Edwardian times they were good stodgy affairs, designed to fill, and this factor became especially important after the Second World War when ingredients were at a premium and all manner of devices were used in order to delude the stomach and taste buds! Wasting food was a sign of bad household management and so if there was any bread left at the end of the week in Midland houses, this would be made into 'Filbelly', the recipe for which consisted of soaked stale bread, sugar, suet, fruit, eggs and mixed spice. Once mixed together, the ingredients were placed into a greased baking tin and baked in the fireside oven for about 2 hours or until nicely browned. Then of course, came the 1970s and with it the prawn cocktail starter, steak and, to finish off, the compulsory Black Forest Gateau or Strawberry Cheesecake – all washed down with a glass or two of Mateus Rosé, Bull's Blood or Blue Nun.

In the 1980s and '90s, there was a change in the attitude of many restaurants and pub owners who began to realize that many of their customers craved for the puddings of their childhood: thus began what can only be described as a revival of some of the more traditional and often regional, dishes such as Jam Roly-Poly, Spotted Dick, Apple Charlotte and Treacle Sponge. In 1985, The Pudding Club was founded at the Three Ways House Hotel, Mickleton, Chipping Campden, Gloucestershire and, in the ensuing two and a half decades, has done much to promote the classic British pudding. So much so, that it has been frequently featured in many magazine and newspaper articles, as well as on television and radio. The owners and managers, Peter Henderson and Jill and Simon Coombe, hold regular Pudding Club 'meetings' at which it is possible to sample the delights of Syrup Sponge, Sticky Toffee Pudding, Gooseberry Fool and Summer Pudding.

Desserts for dinner parties and other special occasions can be different and exciting, but should not cause panic and terror in the heart of the cook. Comforting though a hot pudding may be on a cold winter's evening, hot desserts are not necessarily 'rib-stickers'. Many of the recipes featured here are a result of some very imaginative chefs who have taken the idea of an old-established favourite and made it into something very special; in fact, we would not be guilty of hyperbole to say that they have, as can be seen from the accompanying photographs, in several instances, turned a pudding into an art form.

Apple and Cheddar Cheese Pie

Some northern regions have traditional recipes that mix together sweet and savoury. In Lancashire for instance, an Eccles Cake is incomplete without an accompaniment of Lancashire cheese whilst in Yorkshire, it is common practice to eat a slice of Wensleydale alongside a piece of fruit cake or apple pie. This modern recipe combines the two. Cheddar cheese, traditionally from Somerset, works well, but other cheeses can be tried.

Serves six
700g/1½lb Bramley apples, peeled, cored, quartered and sliced
75g/3oz soft brown sugar
15g/½oz semolina
pinch of ground cinnamon

For the pastry
175g/6oz self-raising flour
50g/2oz wholemeal flour
100g/3½oz butter, chopped into small cubes
75g/3oz mature Cheddar cheese, grated
(retaining a third of this amount to finish the dish)
2 egg yolks
2 dessertspoons water
beaten egg for glazing

Make the pastry by sifting the two flour types into a bowl. Add the butter and two-thirds of the cheese and rub all together until they resemble breadcrumbs. Add the egg yolks and water and mix together until a dough is formed. Wrap in cling-film and chill in the fridge for 1 hour. When thoroughly chilled, roll out three-quarters of the pastry on a lightly floured surface and gently lay the prepared pastry into the bottom of a 23cm (9in) flan dish. Make sure that the pastry comes up all sides of the dish. Spread the semolina over the base before arranging the apple slices and sprinkling the top with sugar and cinnamon. Roll out the remaining pastry to make a lid for the pie and gently lay it over the top, making sure that the connections between lid and pastry sides are well sealed by crimping over the edges between finger and thumb, the handle of a knife or by brushing the edges with milk of beaten egg. Glaze the pastry top with egg and make a small slit in the centre. Bake at 180°C (355°F) for 45 minutes: serve hot and sprinkle the pie with the remaining third of grated cheese just before doing so.

Darleys' Crème Brulée

Bryan and Susan Webb, owners of Darleys' Restaurant, Llandrillo, Corwen, Denbighshire, add their own twist to the classic crème brulée.

Serves six
500ml/16fl oz milk
500ml/16fl oz double cream
130g/4½fl oz caster sugar
200g/7oz egg yolks
2 vanilla pods split lengthways
250g/9oz whimberries

Heat the milk, cream and vanilla pods and leave to infuse for 30 minutes.

In a bowl, lightly whisk the egg yolks and 60g (2oz) sugar until pale, then pour the cream mixture, whisking all the time. Strain into a large jug.

Pre-heat oven to 100°C (210°F). Have ready a large roasting tray lined with a tea towel and place gratin or ramekin dishes in the tray. Add the whimberries and pour in the custard. Place in the oven and pour water around the dishes. Bake for 35–40 minutes until set. Remove from the oven and tray and leave to cool, and then transfer to the fridge. Just before serving, sprinkle the tops of the crème brulée with 70g (2½oz) sugar and caramelize with a blowtorch or under a very hot grill, to make a thin pale nut-brown topping.

Apple Tart – French Style

This might be Apple Tart, but not as you know it! This is a classic British dish that has been given a very definite French twist.

Serves six
1 quantity sweet pastry (*see* below)
250g/9oz crème pâtissière (*see* below)
4 dessert apples
80g/3oz apricot jam

Sweet pastry
350g/12oz plain flour
pinch salt
150g/5oz unsalted butter
100g/3½oz icing sugar
2 eggs, beaten

Sift the flour and salt onto a work surface and make a well in the centre. Put the butter in the well and work it until warm and soft by using your fingertips and thumb in a kind of 'pecking' action. Add the sugar to the butter and incorporate well. Add the beaten eggs to the butter/sugar and mix together. Gradually add the flour from the outsides of the well by flicking it into the mixture and then chopping through it until a rough dough is formed. Finally, bring the whole together using your hands and knead until the rough dough becomes smooth. Wrap in cling-film and cool in the fridge for about 1 hour.

For the crème pâtissière
3 egg yolks
65g/2½oz caster sugar
15g/½oz cornflour
5g/¼oz plain flour
250ml/8fl oz milk
½ vanilla pod
small knob of butter

Whisk together the egg yolks and half the sugar until pale and creamy. Sift in the cornflour and flour and mix together. Put the milk, remaining sugar and the half vanilla pod into a saucepan and bring just to the boil before straining over the egg yolk mixture, stirring continuously. Pour back into a clean saucepan and bring back to the boil (there will most likely be a few lumps in the mixture at first, but they will disappear with some vigorous stirring). Boil for 2 minutes, remove from the heat, stir in the knob of butter (to prevent a skin from forming) and set aside to cool.

To make the apple tart

Roll out the pastry large enough to line a 23cm (9in) round, loose-bottomed fluted tart tin and chill in the fridge for 30 minutes. Blind bake in the oven at 180°C (355°F) – do this by either covering the pastry with a sheet of greaseproof paper and filling it with either real or ceramic baking beans, or using a sheet of kitchen foil, cut as long as the circumference of the baking tin. If choosing the latter method; roll the foil into a long thin strip before coiling it firmly around inside the pastry, pressing it firmly against the sides to make an inner ring. Cook for 10 minutes or until the pastry is dry and just beginning to colour. Remove the paper or foil and check for any cracks that may allow the filling to escape. Patch these up with a piece of leftover pastry (returning the base to the oven for a further 5 minutes), but do not worry about any inconsequential cracks. Use a pastry brush and the egg white left over from making the pastry to coat the whole of the inside of the pastry case – the residual heat will bake it onto the pastry, thus sealing it immediately.

Fill the pastry with the crème pâtissière. Arrange the apple slices over the top of the tart and bake for 25–30 minutes or until the apples are golden and the pastry cooked. Once the tart has cooled, melt the apricot jam in a tablespoon of water and brush over the apples with a pastry brush in order to create an attractive looking, shiny glaze.

Dinca Fala (Apple Cake) with Honey and Clotted Cream

Dinca Fala is a traditional Welsh dish; Mark Freeman, head chef at the Park Plaza hotel in Cardiff, has added a little 'extra' to an accepted recipe. It 'creates a fusion of flavours to suit every palate'.

Serves six

For the cake
280g/10oz self-raising flour
140g/5oz Demerara sugar
140g/5oz unsalted butter
500g/1lb cooking apples, peeled and cut into small pieces
some milk for mixing a dough

To garnish
100g/3½oz clear honey
100g/3½oz clotted cream

Rub the butter into the flour and add the sugar and apples. Mix with enough milk to make a fairly stiff mixture, and then cook in a greased loaf tin at 220°C (430°F) for 30 minutes. Leave to cool and then slice into six slices and serve with a drizzle of honey and a spoonful of clotted cream.

Chunky-Hunky Rice Pudding and Jam

We love rice pudding as, so it seems, do many of the chefs we visited around Britain. This recipe is a home-made version derived from a combination of ideas.

knob of butter
120g/4½oz short grain pudding rice
600ml/1pt milk
85g/3oz brown granulated sugar
125ml/4fl oz single or double cream
1 piece dried orange zest

Butter a shallow pudding dish, sprinkle the rice and sugar evenly across its base, and pour in the milk and cream. Add the orange zest and cook slowly in the oven at 180°C (355°F) for about 1 hour. Serve with home-made plum or rhubarb jam.

Daisy's Chocolate Steamed Pudding

Whilst visiting Sarah Charles at Great Dixter, Northiam, East Sussex, for photos and recipes, we were given details of this wonderfully mouth-watering steamed pudding. The recipe was found in an old, hand-written notebook written by Daisy, the wife of Nathaniel Lloyd; he was at one time the owner of Great Dixter, a medieval estate, whose house was further developed by the architect Edwin Lutyens. Nathaniel's son Christopher was a well-known garden writer and television personality who died in 2006. As well as gardening, Christopher also had a passion for cooking that was obviously inherited from his mother Daisy, apparently a somewhat formidable woman known by some as 'The Management'!

85g/3oz caster sugar (in which a vanilla pod has resided)
85g/3oz butter
3 eggs, separated
85g/3oz chocolate (Menier) melted in a tablespoon of boiling water
100g/3½oz fresh breadcrumbs
60g/2oz un-blanched ground almonds
60g/2oz sultanas

Have steamer ready boiling. Cream butter and sugar; beat in yolks of eggs, singly: then add chocolate, breadcrumbs, almonds and sultanas. If the mixture seems unduly stiff for pouring, add a little milk. Finally, add the egg whites, stiffly whipped.

Pour into a greased pudding basin and cover with a double layer of foil, pleated if the mixture is near to the basin rim. Tie on with a string, secured with a slip knot. Steam for 2 hours. Serve with cream, and away with the killjoys who tell you it's wicked!

Daisy's Chocolate Steamed Pudding . . .

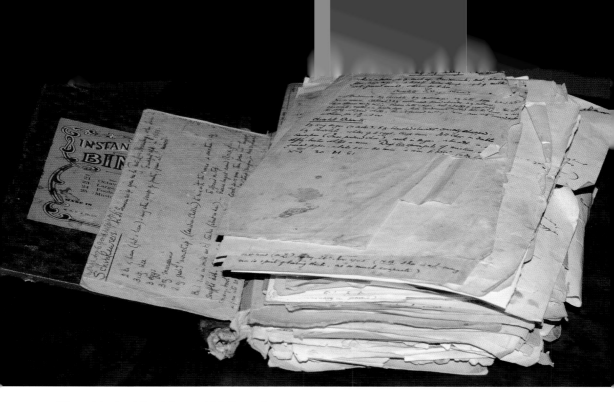

. . . and the original notebook from which the recipe came.

Buckinghamshire Cherry Pasties

Summertime in Buckinghamshire was cherry time. William Hone described the Buckinghamshire Cherry Pasty in his year-book of 1841, stating that, 'those districts have from time immemorial been accustomed to make pasties, which are by them highly esteemed for their delicious flavour; some even considering them fit to set before a king.' In more modern times, the traditional cultivated cherry trees – descended from grafts made from the wild black cherry – and glorying in such names as 'Black Eagle', 'Nimble Dick' and 'Black Bud', are enjoying something of a revival and the fruits produced eagerly seized upon by enthusiastic cooks and restaurateurs.

Makes three large pasties
30–40 cherries, pitted
200g/7oz plain flour
50g/2oz unsalted butter
75ml/2½fl oz water or milk
2 tablespoons caster sugar
½ teaspoon baking powder
egg yolk (save the white for glazing)
pinch of salt

Spoon the flour, baking powder, a large pinch of salt and 1 tablespoon of the caster sugar into a mixing bowl, then add the butter, rubbing in until any lumps disappear. Mix the egg yolk with the milk or water and pour it into the bowl, working the mixture until a softish dough is formed (add a little more liquid if it looks too dry). Leave to one side for about 5 minutes and then knead the dough gently before wrapping it in cling-film and leaving to chill in the fridge for about 1 hour.

Line a baking tray with non-stick baking paper, and pre-heat the oven to 190°C (375°F). Roll the pastry on a lightly floured surface until it is about 30–40mm in thickness, then cut out three discs about 18cm (7in) across (use a side plate as a guide). Place ten or so pitted cherries in the centre of each disc together with the remaining tablespoon of caster sugar. Brush a little cold water around the edge then pinch the edges together with finger and thumb. Glaze the tops of each pasty with a little of the retained egg white and sprinkle over more caster sugar before baking for about 30 minutes or until the juice begins to run. Leave to cool on the tray.

Horlicks Rice Pudding

Another classic pudding given an individual twist is this one from Richard Hughes at The Lavender House, Brundall, Norfolk. He says:

> Rice pudding is a personal favourite. I can still recall eating it cold from the tin when enjoying my days off in digs, not wanting to venture into the hotel for fear of getting roped in to some extra vegetable prepping! This is, however, an altogether different affair, with the addition of your Granny's favourite night-cap to give you that warm cosy glow! If you like the skin on the pudding, bake it in the oven. If not, simmer it on the stove top, stirring frequently, and it'll be done in half the time.

100g/3½oz short grain rice
450ml/16fl oz milk
450ml/16fl oz cream
50g/2oz caster sugar
1 tablespoon Horlicks
40g/1½oz butter
freshly grated nutmeg

Pre-heat the oven to 150°C (300°F). Butter a 1½ltr (3pt) pie dish. Bring the milk and cream to a simmer, and whisk in the Horlicks and sugar. Place the rice in the pie dish, and pour over the milk mixture. Grate on the nutmeg and dot on the remaining butter before baking for 2 hours.

Serve with ice-cream, blackcurrant jam, grilled cinnamon dusted apples, a tot of whisky – whatever takes your fancy!

Horlicks Rice Pudding. (Photo: Richard Hughes at The Lavender House)

No-Fat Christmas Pudding

There can be nothing more traditional than a British Christmas Pudding. At the end of a big main course however, even just a spoonful 'to be sociable' can be too stodgy to enjoy. This updated version provides flavour but no fat and is well worth trying.

NB: Whilst this can be made beforehand, unlike traditional puddings, it will not keep for more than about a fortnight, so don't be too keen to make a start!

1 lemon, juiced and grated
2 medium-sized apples
2 bananas
50g/2oz walnuts
50g/2oz almonds
50g/2oz hazelnuts
450g/1lb mixed fruit
450g/1lb freshly made breadcrumbs
50g/2oz soft brown sugar
4 eggs
150ml/5fl oz milk
1 teaspoon mixed spice
1 teaspoon salt

Don't bother peeling the apples – just grate them and then roughly chop the bananas and nuts. Whisk the eggs into the milk and mix all the ingredients together before stirring well. Place into a 2¼ltr (4pt) well-greased pudding basin and cover with greaseproof paper. Secure in the traditional manner with either rubber bands or string. Steam for 3–4 hours (depending on the size of the bowls being used) in a lidded pan containing approximately 5cm (2in) water, or for about half that time if using a pressure cooker. Remember to check the water level throughout the cooking period. Cool and store until required.

To reheat, steam for 1 further hour or microwave for 6–8 minutes. To serve, run a palette knife around the edges of the bowl before turning out onto a serving dish.

Peterson's Pancake Parcels

Pancakes have always been a traditional way of filling up the hungry countryman without having to resort to ingredients not normally found in and around the farmyard. Dorset head chef, Brian Peterson, uses bananas and home-made apricot jam to fill his pancake parcels. Pressed as to how many the quantities serve, Brian merely stated, 'Well, it depends how thick you like your pancakes!' However, by our reckoning the mixture should make approximately eight pancakes.

For the pancakes
100g/3½oz plain flour
300ml/10fl oz milk
1 egg
pinch of salt
vegetable oil for frying

For the filling
3 bananas, peeled
juice of a lemon
2 tablespoons apricot jam

For the sauce
4 tablespoons undiluted orange squash, made up to 150ml by adding water
2 tablespoons soft brown sugar
25g/1oz butter
½ teaspoon ground cinnamon

Make the pancake batter by sifting together the flour and salt into a bowl and making a well in the centre. Add the egg to the well and gradually add the milk, beating all the time. Leave the pancake mix to stand before heating a little oil in a frying pan until it is very hot. Pour in some of the batter (as Peter says, exactly how much at a time depends on how thick you like your pancakes!), tilting the pan so that the mixture spreads evenly over the entire pan bottom. Cook and turn until both sides are golden-brown. For guests, make all the pancakes and keep them warm (the easiest way is to lay a piece of greaseproof paper between each one and stack them on top of each other as they are cooked). For the family, there's nothing better than making pancakes and eating them immediately they are turned out of the pan!

Mash the bananas together with the lemon juice and jam. Divide the filling equally between the pancakes and then fold each pancake around the filling to form a sort of parcel.

To begin the sauce, pour the diluted juice into a frying pan and add the other ingredients before bringing to the boil, stirring constantly. After about 5 minutes, the mixture should have reduced and become thick and syrupy. Lower the heat, arrange the parcels in the pan, occasionally spooning over the sauce, and cook for about 10 minutes. Serve immediately, with a good spoonful of double or clotted cream.

PANCAKE DAY RACING

Most of today's pancake races are modern institutions, but there is evidence that those at Olney, Buckinghamshire, have been run since 1445. Competitors must be over eighteen years of age, wear skirts, aprons and also have their heads covered. The race ends at the parish church, where the winner is kissed by a member of the clergy, and is followed by the Shriving Service, at which the competitors' frying pans are arranged around the font. Despite this rather strange sequence of events, there is, once the legend of Olney's pancake race has been explained, some logic in these qualifying criteria and subsequent occurrences.

In 1445, an Olney housewife, engrossed in making her pancakes in the lead-up to Lent, made herself late for the Shriving Service. On hearing the bells summoning all parishioners to church, the poor woman panicked and dashed out of the house, pan and pancake in hand, still sporting her apron and mop cap. In honour of this unnamed lady, the Olney race is run only by women who must have lived in the town for a certain period of time. Before the age of political correctness, only true 'housewives' could compete, but nowadays it is possible to stretch the rules.

At exactly five minutes to noon, the women take their places at the starting line located at the Market Place and at the sound of the 'Pancake Bell' the runners toss their home-made pancakes and take off in the direction of the church gate. The starter of the race wears a resplendent, if somewhat historically inaccurate, mixture of a plumed helmet reminiscent of the ones worn in the Napoleonic Wars and a red tunic as worn at the Battle of Waterloo. Whoever reaches the finishing line first can claim their prize – a 'kiss of peace' from the verger and, in addition to the traditional gift of a prayer book, she also receives a number of prizes from local shops and businesses as well as, in recent years, the Liberal prize, which has occurred as a result of a rather unexpected alliance between Olney and an American town. Since 1950 the town of Liberal in Kansas, which has always celebrated Shrove Tuesday with enthusiasm, decided to take a leaf out of Olney's book and stage their own race over the same distance (still traditionally measured at 415 yards). The towns then compare timings and awards are made accordingly.

Harome Honeyed Crème Caramel with Lindisfarne Mead-Soaked Sultanas

Some puddings should be, like Baby Bear's porridge in the story of Goldilocks, not too hot, not too cold, but 'just right!' Andrew Pern, of the Star Inn at Harome, North Yorkshire, tells us:

Mrs Hall, who by chance lives in Honeyholme, provides us with various flavours of her home-made honey, which she collects on behalf of the bees from the surrounding moors and fields. This dessert is partnered with the famous honey beverage of Lindisfarne Mead, made at St Aidan's Winery in the Holy Island – off the rugged coat of Northumberland – it is always a hit with our customers!

Serves two

For the Crème Caramel
330ml/11½fl oz milk
2 egg yolks
2 eggs
25g/1oz caster sugar
25g/1oz Harome honey
5ml/¼fl oz vanilla essence

Harome Honeyed Crème Caramel with Lindisfarne Mead-Soaked Sultanas. (Photo: Andrew and Jacquie Pern at The Star Inn)

Caramel
70g/2½oz sugar
20ml/¾fl oz water
pinch of cream of tartar
10ml/⅓fl oz glucose

First make the caramel, by putting all the ingredients into a pan. Heat, and allow the sugar to dissolve before bringing to the boil. Continue to boil until the sugar turns a deep caramel colour. Pour into moulds straight away and allow to set.

Make the custard, scalding the milk and vanilla on the heat, and add the honey to this.

In another bowl mix the eggs with the egg yolks and sugar (in order to avoid any bubbles forming, don't mix too much in at any one time). Add the custard. Strain the mixture and pour into moulds. Bake in a *Bain Marie*. To protect it from the direct heat, cover the whole *Bain Marie* with foil and bake at 120°C (250°F) for 1 hour and 10 minutes. If you insert a skewer and it comes out clean, then it is ready. Refrigerate and use when required.

For the sultanas
40g/1½oz semi-dried grapes or jumbo sultanas
20ml/¾fl oz mead or a honey liqueur
20ml/¾fl oz liquid glucose or golden syrup

Soak the sultanas in the mead to marinade and use as required. To serve, lightly warm the glucose with a handful of sultanas and also the juice from the mead. Reduce slightly and allow to cool, then spoon around the turned-out crème caramel. Garnish and serve immediately.

Yorkshire Rhubarb and Custard

The great advantage of a cold pudding is that most (but by no means all) can be made earlier in the day, leaving more time for the cook to enjoy time with their guests. From the kitchens of Robert Craggs at the Cadeby Inn, Doncaster, South Yorkshire, this is very definitely *not* the boring old plate of rhubarb and custard you might remember from your childhood!

Rhubarb
500g/1lb Yorkshire rhubarb, cut into 'batons'
100g/3½oz caster sugar
100ml/3½fl oz water
50ml/2fl oz orange juice

Custard
8 free-range egg yolks
40g/1½oz caster sugar
700ml/1¼pt double cream
1 orange, 'zested'

In a stainless steel pan, add the water, orange juice and caster sugar and bring gently to simmer. Add the cut batons of rhubarb and gently poach until tender. Strain and place to one side to cool.

Bring the cream and 'zested' orange to the simmer. Whisk the yolks and caster sugar together before adding the cream to the mix and whisking well. Return to the pan and heat and cook out gently until the custard thickens (do not boil, as this will 'split' the custard). When thick, pass through a sieve and allow to cool. Layer up in glasses as in the accompanying photograph, but always allow each layer to cool before proceeding with the next one.

Rhubarb and Custard Mille Feuille

Like Robert Craggs and his *Yorkshire Rhubarb and Custard*, James Brown of the Ivy, Clifton, York, has produced something with local produce that is subtle-tasting, very different in appearance and not at all like anything that you might normally associate with common-or-garden rhubarb. There's no surprise in the fact that two Yorkshire-based chefs came up with the idea of using rhubarb in their dishes – not only is it seasonal and therefore readily available at the time of year we visited them both, but the area around Wakefield is known as the 'Rhubarb Capital of The World'!

Vanilla Pannacotta
150g/5oz caster sugar
3 leaves gelatine
600ml/1pt double cream
150ml/5fl oz milk
2 vanilla pods

Soak the gelatine leaves in water until soft then squeeze to remove any excess water and set to one side. Add the caster sugar to the gelatine. Bring the milk, vanilla pods and double cream to the boil and then simmer for 5 minutes. Remove the vanilla pods before pouring onto the gelatine and caster sugar mix and whisk until fully dissolved. Put in the fridge and whisk occasionally as it is setting.

Once set, give it a whisk to remove any lumps before placing it into a piping bag.

Orange Tuile
250g/8oz caster sugar
125g/4½oz plain flour
zest and juice of 2 oranges
60g/2oz melted butter

Mix the plain flour and caster sugar together and bind with the orange and butter. Leave to rest for at least 1 hour, but preferably overnight. Spread the mix thinly using a pastry scraper over a rectangle template. Bake at approximately 160°C (320°F) until bubbled and slightly coloured. Leave to set a little once removed from the oven.

Vanilla Anglaise
600ml/1pt double cream
4 vanilla pods
3 egg yolks
250g/9oz caster sugar

Boil the double cream and vanilla. Whisk the eggs and caster sugar until pale. Pour the hot liquid onto them, and stir until all dissolved. Return to a clean pan; cook gently, stirring constantly until thick.

Rhubarb

Cut a quantity of rhubarb into identical 10cm (4in) sticks and steam for approximately 1 minute (depending on the thickness of the rhubarb – they still need to have some 'bite' remaining in them).

Rhubarb 'Granita'
500g/1lb rhubarb
250g/9oz caster sugar
125ml/4fl oz cup water
25ml/1oz vodka

Put the rhubarb, caster sugar and water in a pan and bring to the boil. Simmer until the rhubarb is soft then remove from the heat and pass through a fine sieve. Once cooled, add the vodka. Put in a shallow tray in the freezer and 'rake' occasionally with a fork.

Rhubarb syrup
200g/7oz rhubarb
200g/7oz caster sugar
100ml/3½fl oz water

Put the rhubarb and water into a pan and bring to the boil, simmer until soft. Remove from the heat and pass through a fine sieve. Pour the liquid back into a clean pan, add the caster sugar and simmer to reduce to a syrup. Pour into a 'squeezy' bottle.

Rhubarb and Custard Mille Feuille.

To assemble the *Rhubarb and Custard Mille Feuille*, firstly place an orange *tuile* on the plate. At the two long edges of the *tuile*, place a stick of rhubarb. Pipe the pannacotta into the space between the rhubarb. Repeat this with another layer and then top with another orange *tuile*. Whisk up the vanilla *anglaise* until frothy and pour into a shot glass. Carefully put some of the *granita* onto this. Using the squeezy bottle, decorate by squeezing a line of syrup around the serving plate.

Steve's Sherry Trifle Cheesecake

Steve Waters, head chef at 'M J's', at the Whitehall Hotel, Darwen, Blackburn, likes cheesecake, his wife likes sherry trifle. To keep the both of them happy, Steve developed this particular recipe!

Makes four

For the base
2 eggs
65g/2¼oz caster sugar
65g/2¼oz plain flour
sherry

Steve's Sherry Trifle Cheesecake.

Cheesecake mix
600ml/1pt milk
50ml/2fl oz Bird's custard powder
100ml/3½fl oz caster sugar
350g/12oz cream cheese
150ml/5fl oz cream

Make the sponge base by blending together the eggs and sugar until the mix is white and fluffy; fold in the flour and spoon and smooth into a greaseproof-lined shallow baking tray before cooking at 210°C (410°F) for approximately 12 minutes.

Take a little milk from the 600ml and use it to mix together the custard powder and sugar. Place the remainder of the milk on the hob to boil and, when it has done so, add the custard/sugar mix. Whip the cream whilst the custard is cooking. Pour the custard into the cream cheese, mix and leave to cool. Using a pastry cutter, cut out circles of sponge to fit in the bottom of a mousse ring and soak with sherry. Fold the cream into the cream cheese and custard mix only when it has thoroughly cooled (to aid setting, you could add gelatine. Place two leaves of gelatine into cold water until they become 'rubbery', then put the gelatine in a pan on a little heat). Add the cheesecake mix carefully to the sponge base in the mousse ring and leave to set before removing and serving.

YELLOWMAN

More a type of honey-combed sticky toffee than a pudding, Yellowman is, never-theless a traditional regional dish that can still be encountered in Ireland. To make it, you will need:

500g/1lb golden syrup
250g/9oz brown sugar
1 heaped tablespoon butter
2 tablespoons vinegar
1 tablespoon baking powder

Using a large saucepan, slowly melt together all the ingredients (except the baking powder) and boil it to such a degree that a drop placed in cold water will immedi-ately harden. Stir in the baking powder, at which point life begins to get exciting, as the toffee will foam up due to the vinegar releasing gases from the baking powder. Pour the resultant concoction onto a greased surface and when it has cooled suffi-ciently, fold the edges towards the centre and pull repeatedly until the toffee is a lovely pale yellow colour, after which it should be left in a shallow tray to completely harden. Those with fillings or dentures – beware.

Sparkling Wine Berry Jelly Jewels

Simple but sophisticated, this light summer dessert can be made with any locally produced sparkling wine.

Serves six
1 bottle sparkling wine (or champagne)
150ml/5fl oz water
500g/1lb fresh berries
150g/5oz caster sugar
8 sheets gelatine

Soak the gelatine sheets in water until soft. Gently heat the water, the same amount of sparkling wine and the sugar, stirring until the sugar dissolves. Squeeze out the excess water from the gelatine, add it to the sugar mix and stir until dissolved. Remove from the heat and stir in the rest of the sparkling wine. Fill up six individual large wine glasses with the fruit and pour over the jelly. Refrigerate for a couple of hours before serving.

Almondy Trifle with Raspberries and Chewy Macaroons

Chris Birch is a man on the move! Not only is he a well-known competition cyclist in both the UK and Europe, he is a chef at Frensham, Surrey, where his particular speciality is the creation of all manner of unique puddings. This recipe uses in-season locally grown raspberries.

Serves six

For the macaroons (makes eighteen)
175g/6oz ground almonds
115g/4oz caster sugar
white of 1 large egg
1 teaspoon almond essence

Mix all the ingredients together and roll into 18 small balls. Push them down slightly with your thumb and bake at 160°C (320°F) for 15 minutes (if you prefer them crunchy, bake for 20 minutes).

For the trifle
1 box almond cake slices
500g/1lb mascarpone
2 tablespoons caster sugar
2–3 drops almond essence
2 tablespoons thick double cream
1 large punnet raspberries
almond liqueur

Dice the almond slices and share them between six large wine glasses. Drizzle over a little almond liqueur. Mix the mascarpone, sugar, almond essence and cream together, and, using a dessert spoon, drop a spoonful into each glass. Push down gently and gently scatter some raspberries on top. Place two macaroons on top of the raspberries, spoon on another layer of the cream cheese mix and finish by adding a single macaroon.

Not-So-Traditional Sherry Trifle

At Christmas, everyone's granny used to make a traditional sherry trifle – usually with tinned fruit salad as its base. Instead of using syrupy tinned fruit – generally grown and harvested abroad, which costs much in the way of processing and transportation – try making a trifle at any time of the year using fruits native to the UK, such as gooseberries, blackberries, black and red currants and apples. Unless you are an avid sherry fan, why use it? Country liqueurs that complement the fruit being used make a trifle that is as far removed from that made by granny as it is possible to imagine!

Makes four individual dishes
1 Victoria sponge or Madeira cake
600ml/1pt milk
2 eggs
2 egg yolks
3 tablespoons caster sugar
½ vanilla pod
125ml/4fl oz country liqueur
175g/6oz raspberry or strawberry jam
300ml/10fl oz double or whipping cream
30g/1oz gelatine or jelly cubes
fresh seasonal fruit
almond flakes
mint leaf
small knob of butter
60ml/2fl oz water

First spread the jam onto the cake. Then break the cake into even pieces and lay them on the bottom of individual dessert dishes before sprinkling with liqueur and leaving it to be absorbed by the sponge. Warm the milk and add the vanilla pod. Cover and leave to infuse for 20 minutes then remove the pod. Beat together the eggs, egg yolks and sugar and then add slowly to the milk. Cook over a gentle heat, using a metal hand-whisk to prevent lumps forming. Remove from the heat when the custard starts to thicken and add the lump of butter to prevent a skin forming (occasional stirring will also help to prevent this happening). Leave to cool.

Prepare the fresh fruit by making sure it is clean and sliced or cubed into bite-sized pieces. Place into a saucepan with 60ml (2fl oz) water and sprinkle with a tablespoon of sugar. Warm gently until the sugar dissolves and absorbs the colour from the fruit. Drain (saving the syrup), and place the fruit over the soaked cake mixture.

Take the saved syrup and make a jelly using the gelatine or jelly cubes as per the manufacturer's instructions (it is worth measuring how much liquid you have before adding the thickener as the jelly doesn't want to be too stiff). Pour the jelly over the cake and fruit and leave in a cool place to set.

Pour over the cold custard, whip the cream and spoon carefully on top before garnishing the top with a piece of fruit, almond flakes and/or small mint leaf.

White Chocolate and Baileys Torte with a Summer Berry Compote.

White Chocolate and Baileys Torte with a Summer Berry Compote

Every restaurant seems to indulge the average person's craving for chocolate. The Cottage in the Wood at Malvern Wells, Worcestershire, is no exception! All of the places we have visited have been kind enough to allow us tasting sessions – no wonder then, that, after several months travelling around Britain researching for this book, the reading on the bathroom scales is not the same as it was at the beginning of the year.

For the chocolate torte
150g/5oz dark chocolate
250g/9oz white chocolate
300ml/10fl oz cream
25ml/1fl oz Baileys

Melt the dark chocolate over boiling water. Spread the mix over a sheet of acetate. Turn the coated sheet onto its end and fold the edges together (with the chocolate on the inside) and create a tear-drop shaped 'shell'. Pinch the ends of the sheet and chill in the fridge until set.

Melt the white chocolate over boiling water and cool slightly. Whip the cream until it is at a 'light whip' stage and add a little to the chocolate before adding the mix to the rest of the cream. Add the Baileys liqueur to the mix and pour into the dark chocolate teardrops. Keep in the fridge until required – at which time, remove the acetate sheet and serve with the berry compote.

For the summer berry compote
1 bag red fruit berries
1¼ltr/2pt water
50g/2oz sugar

In the water, boil half the bag of berries and the sugar until a stock/syrup consistency is achieved. Add the remainder of the fruit and allow to cool.

White Chocolate and Basil Crème Brulée

It says much about the British palate that most restaurants we visited or contacted include some sort of chocolate dessert in their menu selection of puddings! Leicester's Restaurant at Laleston, Bridgend, South Wales, is no exception and combines white chocolate with the subtle taste and fragrance of fresh basil.

Serves six
600ml/1pt double cream
100g/3½oz sugar
3oz egg yolk
1 handful white chocolate chips
6–8 basil leaves (depending on taste)

Whisk the yolks and sugar until light and fluffy. Gently bring the cream and basil to the boil. Once boiling, add the egg mix and stir in gently. Slowly bring it back to the boil, stirring all the time. Once the mix starts to thicken and coats the back of the spoon, take off the heat and strain through a fine sieve. Mix in the chocolate. Pour into moulds and leave to set in the fridge for about 2–3 hours. Glaze with caster sugar and serve with a Biscotti biscuit.

Panattoni and White Chocolate Pudding

The White Hart Hotel, Welwyn, Hertfordshire, sometimes has this dessert on the menu – if you're lucky!

1 panattoni bread loaf
300ml/10fl oz milk
300ml/10fl oz double cream
1 vanilla pod
5 eggs
115g/4oz sugar
175g/6oz white chocolate
2 shots Baileys liqueur

Slice the panattoni into slices of about 1cm (¼in) in thickness. Gently heat the milk, cream, vanilla pod and chocolate until the chocolate has dissolved. Allow to cool and add the Baileys. Whisk the eggs and sugar before pouring in the chocolate/cream/Baileys mix and carefully folding all together.

Place layers of the panattoni slices either into loaf tin or individual moulds and between each layer spoon a little of the chocolate cream. Bake at 180°C (355°F) or until set. Serve with vanilla ice-cream and chocolate sauce.

Panattoni and White Chocolate Pudding.

Whites Chocolate Pot

Whites Chocolate Pot

Everything produced at Whites at the Clockhouse, Tenbury Wells, Worcestershire, is made on the premises. Owners Sarah and Chris Whitehead and head chef Jonathan Waters change their menu every month to be sure of utilizing only the very best of in-season local produce – with the exception of their Chocolate Pot, which is so popular that there would be a diners' revolt if it were ever to disappear!

Makes four
60ml/2fl oz double cream
75g/3oz dark 70 per cent chocolate
115g/4oz caster sugar
30ml/1oz water
1 egg
2 egg yolks
zest of ¼ orange
1 teaspoon Cointreau

Melt the chocolate and then heat the sugar with water until it reaches 275°C (530°F) – use a sugar thermometer. Beat the egg yolks and the whole egg until the mix is frothy. Pour in the hot syrup and beat until it cools to luke warm. Beat in the melted chocolate. Add the orange zest. Whip the cream and fold it into the mixture. Pour or spoon into very small individual serving dishes and top off with Cointreau.

Salad of Strawberries with Yoghurt Parfait; Poppy Seed Cake and Basil Ice-Cream

James Holah thinks that 'people eat with their eyes and a "wow" factor is best created with careful preparation and attention to detail.' In this recipe, this talented chef certainly does exactly that.

Poppy seed cake
3 eggs
250g/9oz sugar
150g/5oz poppy seeds
100g/3½oz desiccated coconut
250g/9oz self-raising flour
250ml/8fl oz vegetable oil
250ml/8fl oz natural yoghurt

Bring the eggs and sugar to a peak with a whisk then beat in the poppy seeds, coconut, vegetable oil and natural yoghurt, adding the flour last. Bake in greased dariole moulds at 150°C (300°F).

Yoghurt parfait
15ml/½fl oz water
75g/3oz caster sugar
5 egg yolks
1 leaf of gelatine (soaked in water)
250g/9oz yoghurt
250g/9oz whipped cream

Start the eggs in a whisking machine, bring the water and sugar to 121°C (250°F) in a pan placed on the stove top (test using a sugar thermometer), squeeze out the gelatine leaf and add the sugar syrup then pour onto eggs, whisking until cool. Fold in the yoghurt and, lastly, the cream. Pour into a mould and freeze.

Basil ice-cream
5 bunches basil
500ml/16fl oz milk
500ml/16fl oz cream
250g/9oz egg yolk
150g/5oz sugar

Bring the milk and the cream to the boil; set aside and beat the eggs and sugar together until they peak. Blanch the basil leaves in boiling water until they just start breaking up. Refresh in ice water; then quickly blanch a second time (literally just in and out). Place the basil in a liquidizer and start to blend, adding the milk and cream at the same time. Whisk into the egg/sugar mix before churning in an ice-cream machine.

For the strawberry salad
1 punnet strawberries
cracked black pepper
mint
balsamic vinegar
icing sugar

Slice the strawberries and mix with cracked black pepper, vinegar and icing sugar to taste. Thinly slice the mint and add. Leave for 20 minutes to macerate.

Salad of Strawberries with Yoghurt Parfait and Poppy Seed Cake.

A selection of home-made sorbets (custard, strawberry and lemon).

Hand-Churned Fabulous
Traditional Regional Ice-Creams

Many regional puddings are enhanced by the addition of a locally produced ice-cream. The small market town of Cullompton, in Devon, for example, holds a regular farmers' market at which it is possible to buy buffalo ice-cream and at Chipping in the Forest of Bowland, Lancashire, Robinsons butchers have diversified into producing ice-cream, which is now selling well as far as 20 miles away from the village. In North Yorkshire, the Birchfield family produce ice-cream and sorbets from their herd of pedigree Jerseys, whilst just down the road, it's possible to source freshly made products at Brymor Ice-creams where the milk comes from Guernsey cattle.

Brown Bread Ice-Cream

Gerald Simpson, chef at the Helpin Arms, West Yorkshire, suggested we might like to try this unusual-sounding ice-cream. It was, apparently, very popular in Victorian times, as Gerald discovered in an old cook book – from which he has developed this recipe.

Serves twelve
225g/8oz breadcrumbs
175g/6oz dark sugar
570ml/1pt double cream
285ml/10fl oz fresh milk
4 egg yolks
60ml/2fl oz light rum

Mix the breadcrumbs and sugar in a food processor before pouring them into an open roasting tin and baking them in an oven at 200°C (390°F) for 30 minutes. Turn them occasionally with the aid of a fork. Remove from the oven and leave to cool; process again, but very quickly.

Scald the milk in a saucepan and beat the egg yolks in a bowl. Pour the milk into the eggs, mixing well before returning all to the pan and cooking over a low heat until a thick custard forms. Leave until cold. Meanwhile, lightly whip the cream and stir in the rum. Fold into the custard mix and combine with the breadcrumbs. Freeze in a plastic ice-cream carton or covered Tupperware dish for about 8 hours until firm.

Easy Vanilla Devon Ice-Cream

Equally as famous as its clotted cream, Devon's ice-cream has a rich, creamy texture. Traditionally, the milk came from the South Devon breed of cattle, but any good quality cream will help make this vanilla ice-cream into something you might remember from your childhood holidays along the Devon coastline.

Serves ten
6 medium eggs, separated
125g/4½oz golden syrup
568ml/1pt carton double cream, chilled
seeds from 2 split vanilla pods, or 2 tablespoons vanilla paste

Put egg yolks and syrup into a large bowl. Using an electric hand whisk or freestanding mixer, whisk together for 4–5 minutes until the mixture leaves a ribbon-like trail when you lift the whisk. Pour the cream into a separate bowl and whisk until it begins to thicken and hold its shape, then use a large metal spoon to fold it into the egg mixture. Whisk briefly to combine and then chill. Wash the whisk well. Put the egg whites in a clean, grease-free bowl and whisk until they stand in soft peaks. Using a large metal spoon, add 1 spoonful of egg white to the chilled egg yolk, syrup and cream mixture, and stir thoroughly. Add the remaining egg white and the vanilla seeds or paste – taking care not to knock out the air. Pour the mixture into a large, shallow freezer-proof litre container, then freeze for at least 6 hours until firm. Allow to soften in the fridge for up to 20 minutes before serving.

Turkish Delight Ice-Cream

Uğur Vata of The Galley, Woodbridge, Ipswich, is passionate about the ingredients he uses and the way they are prepared and served. He only uses the best local ingredients were possible. He is a perfectionist and only the highest quality is good enough. He encourages his staff to reach this high standard. In 2008, he was offered the opportunity to open a restaurant in the beautiful marina of Port Gocek, which he is now running to the same high standard as his two restaurants in the UK. One of the specialities of this restaurant in Port Gocek is Uğur fabulous home-made poppy sorbet and Turkish delight ice-cream.

Makes 10 litres!
10ltr/17½pt milk, full fat
2kg/4½lb white sugar
50ml/2fl oz rose water (obtainable from Middle Eastern shops)
25g/1oz ground orchids (also obtainable from Middle Eastern shops – may be known as '*Sahlep*')
a few drops of pink food colouring

Taking care not to let it burn at the bottom of the pan, boil together all the ingredients until the liquid has reduced by a third – this will take about 1 hour. Allow to cool and churn in an ice-cream machine. Spoon into suitable containers and freeze for at least 4 hours before serving. It will keep frozen for about a month.

Hand-turned fabulous Turkish Delight Ice-Cream.

Cinnamon Crumble Ice-Cream Sundae

Similar in method and idea to the *Brown Bread Ice-Cream*, it is, however, very different in taste.

Serves ten
1 tub *Easy Vanilla Devon Ice-Cream*, frozen for 2 hours until starting to firm up.
150g/5 oz plain flour
75g/3oz light muscovado sugar
75g/3oz butter
2 level teaspoons ground cinnamon

To serve
sliced bananas
chocolate sauce
grated chocolate

Pre-heat oven to 190°C (375°F). Put the flour in a large bowl, add the sugar, butter and cinnamon, and rub in the mixture until it looks like crumbs. Spread out the crumble on a non-stick baking sheet and bake for 10 minutes or until golden. Cool for 10 minutes, then break into pea-sized pieces (any larger and the finished ice-cream will be too lumpy; any smaller and they'll disappear) and set aside one-third. Using a wooden spoon, stir the remaining crumble into the ice-cream. Return to the freezer for at least 2 hours until firm. Soften in the fridge for about 20 minutes prior to serving. Put a layer each of bananas, chocolate sauce and ice-cream in tall sundae glasses. Decorate with a sprinkling of reserved crumble and grated chocolate.

Breads, Cakes and Biscuits

There is nothing more British than afternoon tea, and Anna, the Duchess of Bedford, is often credited with its invention. In the early 1800s, when dinner was often not served until 8.30–9.00pm, it is said that the Duchess often became hungry during the period between lunch and dinner. As a consequence, she began ordering small meals to be sent to her private rooms in the late afternoon. After a while, she got rather more brazen and invited her equally 'well-to-do' friends to join her. But a break for a bite of something has also been part of the daily routine for the working classes for just as long, if not longer. Known variously throughout the country as 'bait' or a 'piece', outdoor workers in particular would stop briefly in order to stave off the hunger pangs. Of course, it wasn't possible for farm hands to break off completely in order to go back to the house and so, as can be seen from the many evocative paintings that still abound and the nostalgic writings of the likes of Laurie Lee, a basket of afternoon tea was brought out to them by the farmhouse maid-servant or, on rare occasions, the farmer's wife herself. Today's afternoon teas are still sometimes taken as a 'picnic', but more often than not they are a treat, only to be partaken of when out on a shopping trip, visiting quaint old country towns or, on rare occasions, as an expedition in themselves to world famous venues such as Betty's Tea Rooms in Harrogate, North Yorkshire. There is however, no reason why one shouldn't, on occasion, do as the Duchess of Bedford reputedly did and entertain at home.

Betty's Tea Rooms, Harrogate, North Yorkshire.

~ Breads ~

The trick with any bread or pastry making, as no doubt your Granny will have told you, is to work with cold hands, which will help prevent the dough from sticking to your fingers. If your hands are warm, periodically hold them under the cold tap, drying thoroughly before continuing. When making puff or flaky pastry, if the butter begins breaking through the pastry, or the pastry is becoming warm, stop, wrap and chill for at least 30 minutes. Always work on a floured board and with a floured rolling pin. Once a batch of pastry is made up, it can be kept in the fridge for a couple of days or even frozen until such time as it is needed.

Kentish Huffkin

Unique to Kent, the huffkin is what is known in other places as tea bread. It's about as large as a large powder puff, and with much the same texture, being very light and soft. In any other context we'd call it a roll or bap, but that rather lacks the excitement of the word huffkin. 'The mark of the huffkin', says Martin Flynn, a man who bakes them, 'is the dimple on top. That's what makes it a Kentish huffkin.'

450g/1lb plain flour
15g/½oz fresh yeast (or 1½ teaspoon dried, mixed with a pinch of sugar)
50g/2oz butter, roughly cut
225ml/8oz mixture of milk and water
2 teaspoons sugar
1 teaspoon salt

Blend the fresh yeast with the milk/water mix (if using dried yeast, sprinkle it into the liquid and leave until it becomes frothy in appearance – usually about 15 minutes). Place flour, salt and sugar in a large mixing bowl and rub in the butter before making a 'well' in the centre and adding the yeast liquid. Beat the mixture until it begins to pull away from the sides of the bowl. On a clean well-floured surface, knead the dough until it becomes elastic in texture and glossy in appearance. Place in a clean bowl and encourage it to rise by covering it with a tea-towel and leaving it in a warm place for 1 hour (the airing cupboard is a traditional place with many bread makers). It should, by the end of the hour, have approximately doubled in size.

Shape the dough into one large oval-shaped loaf and place on a greased baking sheet. Cover it again with the tea towel and leave it for a further 30 minutes for it to again double its size. In keeping with Kentish tradition, make a deep thumb mark in the centre of the loaf before baking at 220°C (430°F) for 15–20 minutes or until golden-brown. To keep the crust soft, wrap the loaf in a tea towel whilst it cools.

Irish Herb Garden Bread

This is one recipe where dried herbs are no substitute for fresh, as they cannot provide the herby flavour that makes this bread so delicious.

170g/6oz wholemeal flour
30g/1oz bran
30g/1oz self-raising flour
30g/1oz butter
1 teaspoon baking powder
280ml/10fl oz milk

For the filling
4 dessertspoons chopped parsley
2 dessertspoons marjoram
30g/1oz butter

Pre-heat the oven to 200°C (390°F). Sieve the self-raising flour into a bowl and add the wholemeal flour, bran and baking powder, mixing well. Cut in the fat, then, mixing well, add the milk to the mix in order to form soft but firm dough. Turn out onto a floured baking sheet and shape into a rectangle roughly 15cm × 20cm (6in × 8in). Spread with the chopped herbs mixed with butter before rolling up the rectangle as you would to make a Swiss roll. Place in a 225g (8oz) loaf tin and bake for 20–25 minutes.

Tewkesbury Tea Bread

Although there are many regional variations for traditional tea breads, this one from café owner Tasmin Tate, is different in that it uses self-raising flour rather than yeast.

275g/10oz self-raising flour
225g/8oz caster sugar
175g/6oz currants
75g/3oz sultanas
75g/3oz raisins
300ml/10fl oz strong hot tea
1 egg, beaten

Put the fruits and sugar in a bowl and cover with the tea before leaving to soak. Meanwhile line the base of a 900g (2lb) greased loaf tin and pre-heat the oven to 150°C (300°F). Add the flour and egg to the fruit and tea, and mix together well. Pour into the loaf tin and bake for about 1½ hours. Turn out, cool and serve sliced and spread with butter.

Bara Brith Bread

Bara brith means spotted or mottled and is *the* traditional Welsh teatime cake. Bara brith is usually served spread with butter, but it can be eaten as it is. It may even be toasted and served buttered. As with almost all regional cooking, there are many variations, but this one from Barry Phillips of Bangor, lifts a traditional recipe into something special.

450g/1lb self-raising flour
225g/8oz butter
225g/8oz sugar
¼ teaspoon freshly grated nutmeg
¼ teaspoon mixed spice
pinch of salt
60g/2oz mixed peel
200g/7oz currants
180g/6½oz sultanas
3 eggs
300ml/10fl oz hot tea
6 tablespoons milk
1 tablespoon marmalade
1 tablespoon golden syrup

First prepare the strong tea and then pour it over the fruit in a bowl before covering and leaving to stand over night. Sift the flour into a bowl, add the spice and nutmeg and a pinch of salt. Cut the butter into small cubes, add to the flour and rub in until the flour and butter are thoroughly mixed. Remove the fruit from the tea and add it to the butter and flour mixture. Tip in the sugar and mix well. Beat the eggs and milk together and add this to the mixture. Finally, add the marmalade and golden syrup and mix thoroughly. Grease a 500g (1lb) bread or baking tin with butter, line with baking parchment and pour in the cake mixture. Bake in an oven pre-heated to 170°C (340°F) for 15 minutes. At the end of this time take the cake out, line the top with baking parchment (to prevent the top burning) and return to the oven for a further 20 minutes (at this point check the bread occasionally – it is ready when set in the middle and golden-brown in colour).

Lincolnshire Plum Bread

Such is the increasing popularity of Lincolnshire Plum Bread that it is being made in other counties and sold under the same name. Like champagne which, under EU law, cannot be called 'champagne' unless made in that particular region of France, the bakers of Lincolnshire want their plum bread protected by similar laws. The EU has already given protected status to thirty-six regional British foods (including Stilton cheese) and, if the producers of this particular bread have their way, Lincolnshire Plum Bread could be added to the list. Make a version of it now, whilst you legally can!

450g/1lb strong white flour
225g/8oz prunes, cut into small pieces
115ml/4fl oz milk, warm
110g/4oz butter, melted
4 tablespoons sugar
50g/2oz currants
50g/2oz sultanas
15g/½oz 'easy-blend' yeast
2 eggs, lightly beaten
1 teaspoon ground cinnamon
1 teaspoon ground all-spice
pinch of salt

Mix milk, sugar, butter, yeast, beaten egg, salt, and spices. Add the flour, beating until smooth and a soft pliable dough is formed. Turn out onto floured surface and knead until smooth and elastic. Place in greased bowl, cover and allow to stand in a warm place until the mixture has doubled in volume. Knock back and knead briefly, adding the dried fruits, ensuring they are evenly distributed. Divide the dough in two, place into two 450g (1lb) greased and lined loaf tins. Cover and leave in a warm room to rise until doubled in size. Pre-heat oven to 190°C (375°F) before baking on a pre-heated baking sheet for 40–50 minutes. Remove the loaves from the tins and return them to the oven for 5–10 minutes or until, when tapped on the base, they sound hollow.

Michael B White's Special Bread

East Sussex artist Michael B White exhibits oils, watercolours, etchings and pastels throughout the world. His wife Sarah Charles is an exhibition designer and has also designed this particular recipe because she doesn't like to eat wheat or too much salt. 'This is a heavy, chewy bread, fulfilling, and great toasted!'

100g/3½oz yeast
400ml/14fl oz lukewarm water
15ml/½fl oz tablespoon sea salt
15ml/½fl oz tablespoon liquid honey

Combine all the ingredients together in a large bowl at room temperature (use a large balloon whisk to mix well together). Keep in a draught-proof but warm area with cloth over the top of the bowl and allow to stand for 15 minutes until the mix becomes bubbly. Mix in the following ingredients in this order:

1 beaten egg
400g/14oz rye flour
125g/4½oz soya flour
100g/3½oz coarse oatmeal
45ml/1½fl oz olive oil
150ml/5fl oz warm milk
45ml/1½fl oz lemon juice
25g/1oz hemp seeds
100g/3½oz sunflower seeds
100g/3½oz pumpkin seeds

Michael B White's Special Bread.

Cover the bowl with a cloth again, keep in a warm draught-free area, and allow to rise for about 1 hour. Turn the dough out onto a well-floured surface. Rub flour onto your hands and then knead the dough lightly for not more than 5 minutes. Cut the dough into two and shape into round or oval loaves. Place on a baking sheet set on an oven tray. Cover with a cloth and leave to rise again for 25 minutes. Scatter and push a handful of mixed pumpkin and sunflower seeds into the top of the loaves. Brush the tops with milk, cut a cross into the top of each – or long diaginal cuts along the length. Bake on the lowest rack in the oven for 35–40 minutes at 200°C (390°F). When the loaves are cooked, tapping them on the base will produce a hollow sound. Leave them to cool on a wire rack.

NB: When baking any bread, do not be tempted to open the oven during cooking times or your bread will fail to rise. Bread does not react well to any draughts in your kitchen whilst you are preparing it. Utensils, bowls and all ingredients at a warm room temperature will aid a successful bake.

Aberdeen Rolls (Buttery Rowies)

Use these traditional Scottish 'baps' to wrap around any sandwich filling, but why not create a theme by including a thick slice of carefully roasted cold meat carved from an Aberdeen Angus joint?

Makes approximately 16 rolls
450g/1lb strong plain flour
170g/6oz butter
175g/6oz lard
1 heaped teaspoon salt
2 heaped teaspoons sugar
25g/1oz fresh yeast (or 1 tablespoon dried)
150ml/5fl oz tepid water

Mix the yeast, sugar and half the water in a small bowl and leave for 15 minutes. Sieve the flour and salt into a large bowl before adding the yeast. Mix the ingredients together with enough water to make a smooth firm dough. Transferring the dough to a well-floured surface, knead it well for about 5 minutes. Place the dough back into the bowl, cover with a warm slightly damp cloth and set aside in a warm place for about 1 hour or until it is roughly double its original size. While the dough is rising, cream together the butter and lard and, when the dough has risen, knead it again before rolling it out on a floured surface. Spread it with a third of the butter and lard mixture and sprinkle lightly with flour. Fold the dough in three and roll it out again. Repeat the procedure twice more. Roll out the dough quite thinly and cut into squares. Bring the four corners of each square to the centre, shape them into rounds and flatten slightly with the ball of your hand (taking care not to over handle the dough). Place the uncooked rolls onto a floured and warm baking tray and leave them in a warm place to rise for about 30–40 minutes. Bake in a pre-heated oven at 230°C (445°F) for about 15–20 minutes until golden-brown and crispy on both sides.

Welsh Leek and Sage Bread

At one time, almost every Welsh village was in close proximity to a watermill that ground local oats and provided wheat and barley flours. Stone-ground flour is, once again, becoming a popular commodity and can be found in many local health food shops and farmers' markets throughout Britain.

240g/8½oz strong white flour
240g/8½oz strong wholemeal flour
15g/½oz dried yeast
1 teaspoon salt
1 teaspoon dried sage, crumbled
1 large leek, chopped
30g/1oz butter
300ml/10fl oz lukewarm milk
1 teaspoon sesame seeds
black pepper

Melt the butter in a pan and use to sweat the leeks. Meanwhile add the flours, yeast, salt, black pepper and sage to a large bowl. Form a well in the middle and add the leeks and the warm milk. Work into the flour until it comes together as a dough that begins to leave the side of the bowl. Place onto a lightly floured surface and knead for 10 minutes until silky. Put the worked dough in a fresh, lightly greased bowl, cover with a tea towel and set aside in a warm spot until nearly doubled in size. Tip the dough onto a floured surface, knock back and knead for 10 minutes more. Cut the dough in half and shape into two round loaves. Place these on a lightly greased baking tray, brush with a little milk and scatter the sesame seeds over the top.

Cover the loaves with a tea towel and place in a warm spot to double in size (about 40 minutes) then place in an oven pre-heated to 200°C (390°F) and bake for about 30 minutes. When the bread is ready it should be golden-brown in colour and will sound hollow when tapped on its base. Transfer to a wire rack and allow to cool.

Speckled Celtic Bread

As its name suggests, this bread, with regional variations, originates from Scotland, Wales and Ireland, but it deserves to be enjoyed everywhere! Eat it either on its own, spread with butter or, as Michael Barry suggests in his book *Radio Times Cookery Year* (Network Books, 1994), 'toasted, buttered and sprinkled with a little cinnamon to make that old-fashioned and oft forgotten treat – cinnamon toast.'

450g/1lb strong white flour
1 sachet dried yeast
300ml/10fl oz warm water
50g/2oz butter
100g/3½oz mixed fruit
25g/1oz caster sugar
½ teaspoon each of ground cinnamon, ground all-spice and salt
1 tablespoon milk
3–4 drops olive oil

Mix together the flour, salt and dried yeast; add the water and knead everything together with your hand until a firm dough is formed. Smear the mixing bowl with the oil, turn the dough in the oil, cover with a clean tea towel and set aside in a warm place until it has risen and approximately doubled in size (45–60 minutes). On a floured board, knock it back using the ball of your hand and add the butter, fruit, spices and most of the sugar. Work the dough until all are thoroughly mixed. Place in a greased loaf tin and set aside in a warm place until the mixture has risen once more. When the dough is showing higher than the sides of the tin, brush the top with the milk and sprinkle with the remaining caster sugar. Bake at 220°C (430°F) for 45 minutes before removing from the tin and leaving to cool on a rack. As with all breads, a sure-fire way to check that the loaf is properly baked is to tap the bottom – if it sounds 'hollow', it is ready, if not, return the loaf to the turned-off oven and leave it (out of its tin) for a further 10 minutes.

Ulster Soda Bread

Soda bread is delicious eaten with butter and jam on the day it is made or toasted or warmed in the oven or microwave for the subsequent few days. It is the perfect accompaniment to a cooked breakfast, makes great sandwiches and is also great served as an accompaniment to a stew or casserole.

250g/9oz plain flour
1 teaspoon salt
1 teaspoon bicarbonate of soda
2 teaspoon soft brown sugar
225ml/7fl oz buttermilk or live yoghurt
olive oil or lard, for greasing

Pre-heat the oven to 230°C (445°F). Grease a baking sheet with a little oil or lard. Sift the flour, salt and soda into the mixing bowl and add the sugar before stirring in the buttermilk or yoghurt, at first with a wooden spoon, then bringing it all together in a doughy mass with your hands (it should feel soft and firm, not sticky – add a little more flour if the mixture is too wet). Knead the dough lightly in the bowl for about 30 seconds until smooth, and then shape it into a ball. Place it on the greased baking sheet. Slash a deep cross in the top of the loaf with a sharp knife. This will allow the bread to open out as the soda starts to work and expand the dough. Bake in the oven for about 12 minutes; turn the oven down to 200°C (390°F) and cook for another 15–20 minutes, until the base of the bread sounds hollow when you tap it. Allow the bread to cool for 15 minutes, then cut it into thick slices and serve.

Tyne Valley Flat Bread

This recipe makes a good lunch dish when served hot with a salad made from flat-leaf parsley, olive oil and thinly sliced red onion.

Makes two
700g/1½lb Ciabatta flour
4 tablespoons olive oil
7g/¼oz 'fast-action' yeast
425ml/15fl oz warm water
1 teaspoon salt
fresh thyme, finely chopped
4 potatoes, thinly sliced

Make a dough by mixing together all the ingredients, except the potatoes, and knead together well for 10 minutes. Wrap in cling-film and place in the fridge overnight. Cut the dough in half and stretch into two large rounds and place on oiled baking sheets. Put the potato slices on the top of the two loaves, brush with olive oil and scatter over some thyme. Bake at 200°C (390°F) for 20–25 minutes or until the base of the loaves sound hollow when tapped and the potatoes are tender.

Cornish Hevva Bread

Probably as well-known as Cornish pasties; apart from the addition of fruit and the fact that several hundred miles separate the regions, Hevva Cake is not dissimilar to *Aberdeen Rowies*. Sometimes rather unappetizingly known as 'heavy cake', tradition has it that it was taken by fishermen as part of their packed lunch and is said to get its name from the word 'hevva' – the cry of the fisherman's look-out man upon seeing a shoal of pilchards.

450g/1lb plain flour
115g/4oz lard
115g/4oz butter
170g/6oz sugar
340g/12oz sultanas
150ml/5fl oz milk
pinch of salt
1 egg (beaten)

Rub the salt and the lard into the flour until it looks like breadcrumbs. Add the sugar and the sultanas and mix well. Add the milk and mix with a knife into a firm dough. Place on a floured board and roll into a long strip. Take a third of the butter and dot the strip two thirds of the way down. Fold the strip one third down and then one third up. Repeat the folding, buttering and rolling three times, and on the third time fold the strip out to fit your baking tray. Mark strip into squares and glaze with beaten egg. Bake in oven at 180–200°C (355–390°F) for about 30 minutes.

~ CAKES ~

Visit any farmers' market or country produce stall at one of the many rural events held throughout Britain and the biggest crowds will always be found around where cakes are being sold. The fact that many people prefer to buy their cakes rather than make them is perhaps not surprising as, unlike any other forms of cooking, cake-making has always been considered a precise art, requiring careful weighing of ingredients and an almost constant watch over the oven as the cake is baking. However, home baking has never been easier, due in part to the advent of mixers, processors and the easy availability of quality ingredients. Although it is impossible to give recipes for all the cakes originating from every region of Britain, the few that follow will make the perfect accompaniment to afternoon tea. In addition, look out for recipes elsewhere that suggest their place of 'birth'. For example: Devonshire Apple Cake and Dundee Cake.

Flour-Free Raspberry Sponge

A recipe for a good cake that is not made from flour is always handy for those with a wheat intolerance or allergy.

6 eggs, separated
250g caster sugar
350g ground almonds
1 teaspoon baking powder

Whisk the six egg whites until stiff and set to one side. In another bowl, whisk the egg yolks and caster sugar together, but not to the point where it becomes very pale and thick. Into this, gently fold the egg whites in three portions, followed each time by a third of the ground almonds and a third of a teaspoon of baking powder, mixing until all are evenly incorporated. Divide the mixture between two 20cm (8in) greased cake tins and give them a couple of gentle taps on the worktop in order to bring up any air bubbles. Bake in a pre-heated oven for 35 minutes at 190°C (375°F), or until the tops feel springy to the touch and the sides are shrinking away from the tin. Turn them out and leave them to cool on a wire rack. Sandwich the two sponges together with raspberry jam worked until smooth. If in season, gently stir in some fresh raspberries with the jam. Finally, dust the top with icing sugar.

Dyllis's All-Bran Cake

Whilst travelling around Britain visiting restaurants in connection with this book, we stayed at some wonderful bed and breakfast places found on the 'Farm Stay UK' website. All participants are working farms and it was a great opportunity to meet some wonderful people, many of whom helped us in our research and even, as in the case of Dyllis Hatch at Goose Green Farm, Mottram St Andrews, Cheshire, gave us a recipe or two of their own. Dyllis says that this cake is to be sliced and eaten with butter. It keeps well in a tin and can also be frozen without losing any of its flavour. She told us that it is so popular with guests that she often 'batch bakes' in groups of four and that her cakes have travelled to Alaska, New Zealand and Australia! It was, apparently, developed from a Women's Institute recipe.

1 cup self-raising flour
1 cup All-Bran
1 cup sugar
1 cup raisins
1 cup milk
a few glacé cherries
pinch of salt

Soak the All-Bran, sugar and raisins in the milk for at least 1 hour, then add the cherries, salt and flour before mixing thoroughly. Place in a greased 225g (8oz) loaf tin and cook in a pre-heated oven at 180°C (355°F) for about 1 hour.

NB: To save greasing the loaf tin (and having to clean it afterwards!), Dyllis suggests using greaseproof loaf tin liners available from Lakeland Plastics.

Dyllis's All-Bran Cake.

Mrs Taylor's Quick-Boiled Fruit Cake

Like the recipe for *Dyllis's All-Bran Cake*, this fruit cake keeps particularly well. The recipe was given to me several years ago by an old lady I used to visit in Cranleigh, Surrey. Whether it is a Surrey recipe I do not know, but it was, according to Mrs Taylor, very popular when she was first married. As she was in her eighties when I used to visit her and that was in the late 1970s, it's safe to say that it's been around for a while.

225g/8oz self-raising flour
225g/8oz raisins
225g/8oz sultanas
175g/6oz currants
175g/6oz glacé cherries, chopped
150g/5oz margarine
2 teaspoons mixed spice
1 teaspoon ground cinnamon
2 eggs
400g/14oz can condensed milk

Pre-heat the oven to 150°C (300°F). Lightly grease and line a 18cm (7in) deep round cake tin with greaseproof paper, which has been further 'greased'. Pour the can of milk into a heavy-bottomed pan, add the margarine, fruit and cherries before placing over a low heat until the condensed milk and margarine have melted. Stir well and then simmer gently for a further 5 minutes. Remove and set aside to cool, but as it does so, give the mixture an occasional stir.

Place the flour and spices into a large mixing bowl. Make a 'well' in the centre; add the eggs and the cooled mixture from the pan, quickly mixing all with a wooden spoon or spatula until properly blended. Turn into the round cake tin and bake for around 1¾–2 hours or until the cake is obviously done – the top should feel firm when gently pressed and the colour should be golden-brown. After removing from the oven, leave the cake to cool for a short while (about 10 minutes) before turning out onto a cooling tray.

Flourless Chocolate Cake

Like the recipe for *Flour-Free Raspberry Sponge*, this cake is made without flour. It is, however, considerably richer, especially when served with a large spoonful of whipped cream!

225g/8oz plain chocolate
225g/8oz unsalted butter, cubed and softened
280g/10oz caster sugar
5 eggs

Break the chocolate into a large mixing bowl and stand over a pan of gently simmering water until it has all melted. After removing from the heat and allowing to slightly cool, beat the butter into the chocolate. Add the sugar and continue beating until the ingredients are well blended. In another bowl, beat the eggs until frothy and then fold them into the chocolate/butter/sugar mix. Grease a cake tin approximately 22cm (9in) in diameter and 4cm (1½in) deep and pour in the cake mix before placing it in a second cake tin bigger than the first. In the second tin, pour water until it reaches about 2.5cm (1in) up the outside of the first one. Bake in a pre-heated oven at 180°C (355°F) for 1 hour and then let the cake completely cool whilst still in the baking tin. Remove it from the water-filled tin and chill it in the fridge overnight. When required, run a round-bladed knife around the edge of the tin and turn it onto a plate.

Rich Chocolate Cake and Cinnamon Cream Filling

This particular chocolate cake recipe uses wholemeal flour. Cakes made with wholemeal flour are generally more substantial than those made with ordinary white flour – don't expect to move too far after eating a slice or two of this one.

170g/6oz wholemeal flour
225g/8oz unsalted butter
85g/3oz fine Demerara sugar
(made 'fine' by drying in a low oven before being 'whizzed' in a blender)
85g/3oz Muscovado sugar
55g/2oz cocoa powder
4 eggs, well-beaten
2 teaspoons baking powder
1 heaped teaspoon honey

For the cinnamon filling
140ml/5fl oz fresh double cream
1 teaspoon fine Demerara sugar
½ teaspoon ground cinnamon

Line the bottom of two 20cm (8in) sandwich tins with baking parchment and grease and flour the sides. Sift the flour with the cocoa and baking powder into a bowl. In another bowl, cream the butter and sugar until light and fluffy and then add the eggs alternately with the flour, mixing well after each addition. Finally stir in the honey. Divide the mixture between the cake tins and bake in an oven pre-heated to 200°C (390°F) for about 20–25 minutes. When the cakes have cooled slightly, turn them out onto wire cooling trays and peel the baking parchment from the bottom of each. Whip together the three ingredients for the cinnamon filling until firm. Sandwich together with cinnamon cream and dust the top with icing sugar. For special occasions, decorate further by icing the sides and top with more cinnamon cream or a coffee icing and the top with shards of grated chocolate.

Shelly's Scones

Neither of the authors are sure where a scone recipe should be placed – is it a type of bread or is it a cake? Nevertheless, we have decided to put Michelle Butterworth's recipe here. Baked in 'Cromwell', the Aga (*see* page 82), they appear from personal tasting to be just perfect!

50g/2oz butter or margarine
225g/8oz self-raising flour
25g/1oz sugar
50g/2oz sultanas
150ml/5fl oz milk
pinch of salt
egg wash

Sieve the flour with a pinch of salt; add the fat, sugar and sultanas. Bring all together with a drop of milk (and/or egg, if preferred). Roll out to a thickness of 3.8cm (1½ in) before cutting into rounds with a pastry cutter. Place the rounds on a greased baking tray before brushing with the egg wash. Cook in the top of 'Cromwell' (or a medium oven!) for approximately 20–30 minutes. Serve with as local a double or clotted cream as you can get and a dollop of home-made jam from the nearest neighbour!

Shelly's Scones.

Lavender Scones

Sarah Charles is a firm believer in using natural and organic products, but warns: 'When making these scones, be careful to use English lavender (*Lavandula officinalis*) rather than French lavender (*Lavandula stoechas*), which is toxic!'

Makes twelve scones
250g/9oz self-raising flour
2 teaspoons baking powder
100g/3½oz caster sugar
1 level teaspoon dried or fresh English lavender
110g/4oz butter
280ml/10fl oz milk
juice of ½ a lemon

Pre-heat the oven to 160°C (320°F). Mix the dry ingredients in a bowl with the lavender and rub through the butter to form a fine breadcrumb effect. Add the lemon juice and milk and mix together (the mixture should be quite wet). Put it on a well-floured board and knead it for 30 seconds until it is floured enough to work with (it should still, however, remain moist inside). Shape into flattish round and cut into shapes with a floured cutter. Bake in the oven for 12–15 minutes. Remove from the oven and leave to cool on a wire rack. Serve with clotted cream and home-made strawberry, greengage or fig jam.

Lavender Scones.

Ripon Spice Loaf

Although called a loaf, the fact that this recipe from Ripon, North Yorkshire, uses fruit and spices and can be served sliced and buttered in the manner of *Dyllis's All-Bran Cake*, made us include it here, rather than at the beginning of this section.

Makes two loaves
450g/1lb self-raising flour
275g/10oz sugar
225g/8oz butter
3 eggs, beaten
225g/8oz currants
225g/8oz raisins
50g/2oz glacé cherries, chopped
50g/2oz mixed peel, chopped
50g/2oz ground almonds
1 tablespoon mixed spice
1 tablespoon baking powder
150ml/5fl oz fresh milk

Pre-heat oven to 150°C (300°F) and grease and line two 900g (2lb) loaf tins before creaming together the butter and sugar until pale and fluffy in texture. Gradually add the beaten eggs and stir in the milk, fruit and almonds before finally folding in the remaining ingredients. Divide the mixture between the two loaf tins and bake for between 1½–2 hours or until the top looks browned and the loaves are coming away from the sides of the tin. Allow to cool in the tins and then turn out onto a wire tray.

Funeral Cake

This is a rich fruit cake traditionally served with teas after a funeral and variations to this recipe can be found all over Britain. Despite its morbid-sounding name, it is a good cake to be served at any time!

240g/8½oz plain flour
1/4 tsp baking powder
240g/8½oz sugar
240g/8½oz mixed dried fruit
1 teaspoon mixed spice
1 egg, beaten
a little milk for mixing

Mix all the dry ingredients together then add the egg. Mix thoroughly and begin adding the milk a little at a time (the eventual consistency needs to be that of a cake batter). Tip the batter into a greased loaf pan and place in an oven pre-heated to 160°C (320°F). Bake for about 1 hour, or until the cake is nicely coloured and a skewer inserted into the centre of the cake emerges cleanly. Allow to cool on a wire rack before slicing and serving with plenty of butter.

TWELFTH NIGHT CAKE

5 January: Twelfth Night marks the end of the Christmas period. In the British Isles it was usual to make a simple fruit cake to be eaten at this time and superstition dictated that it should contain some good luck charms or 'favours' such as cloves, twigs or even a piece of rag. The most common addition to the cake mix was, however, a bean and a pea; whoever got the bean was 'king' for the night and the recipient of the pea, the 'queen'. For the rest of the evening, they ruled supreme and, even if they were normally servants in daily life, their temporarily exalted position was acknowledged by their masters. To make sure that a member of the right sex received the correct favour a bean was placed in one half of the cake and a pea in the other during baking – as the visitors arrived, ladies were served from the left-hand 'pea' side, men from the right. Whatever happened if a male got the pea, or a female the bean, is not recorded.

There was a more serious reason for the inclusion of the bean, as the person who found it in their piece of cake was considered to be a sort of guardian angel for that particular family for the forthcoming year, so it was often arranged that a senior family member would receive the 'gift'.

When Twelfth Night feasting was banned by the Puritans in the sixteenth century, the custom of baking a cake died out to a certain extent, but the practice continued in some areas of the British Isles until the early part of last century, only to be eventually replaced by the Christmas cake as we know it today.

The cake was also sometimes known as an Epiphany cake and a piece given to the local priest who would visit and bless each house in his parish on 6 January.

Despite the disappearance of the Epiphany cake in the UK, it is still an important part of the Christmas/New Year tradition elsewhere in Europe, especially in France where the *gateaux* or *galette des Rois* is found in every village bakery. Nowadays a small pottery figure takes the place of the bean and each cake is supplied with a gold paper crown.

The colour of cider cake will vary depending on the variety of apples being used.

Herefordshire Cider Cake

Cider cake is famously baked in Herefordshire due to its association with local cider-apple growing, but other cider-producing counties also make a version of the cake. Depending on the variety of apple used, you might find that the interior of the cake has a slightly pinky and very attractive colour to it.

125g/4½oz butter, diced
125g/4½oz sugar
2 eggs, beaten
225g/8oz self-raising flour
1 teaspoon bicarbonate of soda
½ teaspoon of grated nutmeg or ground cinnamon
200ml/7fl oz cider
caster sugar for sprinkling

Grease a square, shallow cake tin and pre-heat oven to 180°C (355°F). In a large bowl, cream together the butter and the sugar until light and fluffy. Gently fold in the beaten eggs. Into another bowl sift the flour, the bicarbonate of soda and the spices. Fold half of the flour mixture into the creamed butter.

Add the cider and mix thoroughly. Stir in the remaining flour, and as soon as mixed turn into prepared tin. Bake for about 35–40 minutes. Allow to cool in tin, and sprinkle with caster sugar once turned out.

GÂCHE CAKE

Despite having chosen loyalty to the English crown at the time of the Norman invasion, the Channel Islands, and in particular, Guernsey, have many French words in their vocabulary and there is still a *patois* spoken by some of the island's older residents. *Gâche* is a kind of bread/cake, but confusingly, any kind of pastry can also be called *gâche*: apple tarts, for example, are called *gâche à pommes*. The traditional Guernsey Gâche is made from plain flour, butter, eggs, candied orange peel, sultanas, milk, brown sugar and yeast. It is, or was, according to those in the know, 'best served with cider from the jug, whilst out hay making.'

~ BISCUITS ~

Biscuits are easy to make and the more uneven the shape, the more interesting each one looks! Whilst they can be uneven in shape, they should, however, be even in thickness, otherwise as they cook, the thinner ones will be ready (and even burnt) before the thicker ones are cooked right through. Remember to place each biscuit mix well away from its neighbours on the baking tray, as they have a habit of spreading! Generally, in a normal oven (as opposed to fan-assisted), it is best to bake biscuits in the centre, as this helps to give them even baking and colouring. When baking two trays (as is the case in several of these recipes), put one tray on the shelf above the other and, halfway through the baking time, change over the trays.

In hot weather, a biscuit mixture containing a high proportion of fat to flour may become too soft to handle easily – in which case the best thing to do is to wrap it in clingfilm and place it in the fridge for 30 minutes or so before continuing to work with it.

Brandy Snaps

As a child brought up in the north of England, I always remember going to the annual Easter Fair and being overwhelmed by the heady smell of candy floss and brandy snaps. My grandfather counted brandy snaps as a rare indulgence, but nowadays, the mixture is fashionable in creating a 'basket' base for sophisticated desserts. Traditionally, however, brandy snaps were served in the form of a tube made by wrapping the mixture around the handle of a wooden spoon. Fill them with freshly whipped double cream for a real treat!

Makes sixteen
50g/2oz butter
50g/2oz granulated sugar
65g/2½oz golden syrup
50g/2oz self-raising flour
2 teaspoons lemon juice
1 teaspoon ground ginger

Put butter, sugar and syrup into a saucepan and place over a low heat until melted. Sift together the flour and ginger and add to the melted mixture, together with the lemon juice. Drop 20ml (¾fl oz) of the mixture (well apart to allow for spreading) onto a greased baking tray. Bake at 170°C (340°F) for 8 minutes. Leave for 1 minute and then lift off the tray with the aid of a palette knife before rolling quickly and loosely around the greased handle of a wooden spoon. Leave until firm and then slide off the handle. Repeat the process with the remaining mixture.

Scottish Oatcakes

Traditionally, oatcakes are cooked on a griddle, but most cooks nowadays use a conventional oven. For a sweeter oatcake than this particular recipe makes, add two teaspoons of sugar to the dough.

Makes a dozen biscuits
100g/3½oz fine oatmeal (plus a little extra for rolling)
15g/½oz lard
150ml/5fl oz water
pinch of salt
pinch bicarbonate of soda

Place the measured oatmeal, salt and bicarbonate of soda into a bowl before gently heating the lard and water until the fat has melted. Pour sufficient of the lard/water liquid into the bowl of dry ingredients to make a firm dough. Roll out the dough on a board sprinkled with oatmeal until it is about 0.3cm (⅛in) thick. Using a 7.5cm (3in) cutter, cut out twelve rounds, re-rolling as necessary (alternatively, cut into triangles if preferred). Place on a greased baking sheet and bake at 180°C (355°F) for 30 minutes or until they are obviously crisp and done.

Dorchester Biscuits

Thanks again to café owner Tasmin Tate for this unusual and tasty regional biscuit recipe.

Makes thirty biscuits
100g/3½oz plain flour
100g/3½oz Cheddar cheese, grated
100g/3½oz softened butter
50g/2oz mixed nuts, chopped
pinch of salt
¼ teaspoon cayenne pepper

Place all the ingredients – with the exception of the nuts – into a bowl and, using a palette knife, work them together. Form a dough by using your hands and then roll into small balls about the size of a walnut. Place the balls on two greased baking trays and sprinkle the chopped nuts over before gently flattening the balls with your hand. Bake at 180°C (355°F) for 15–20 minutes (they should be golden-brown in colour). Cool on a wire rack.

Grasmere Gingerbread

The ancient custom of rush-bearing still continues in five Cumbrian churches: at Grasmere, Ambleside, Great Musgrave, Urswick and Warcop. A local band leads a procession of adults, girls wearing floral crowns and boys carrying rush crosses, from the village reading rooms through the village and, after stopping for refreshments, ends at the church with hymns and prayers. Traditionally the children are given a piece of Grasmere gingerbread if they have carried one of the rushes.

500g/1lb1oz fine oatmeal
250g/9oz Muscovado sugar
250g/9oz butter
2 tablespoons golden syrup
4 teaspoons ground ginger
1 teaspoon all-spice
½ teaspoon baking powder

Line a Swiss-roll or baking tin with greaseproof paper and grease it well. Stir the dry ingredients together. Melt the butter and syrup over low heat, pour on to the dry ingredients and stir well to make a fairly stiff mixture. Spread the mixture evenly over the base of the prepared tin and bake at 180°C (355°F) for 25–30 minutes (don't be alarmed by the fact that the mixture will look a little runny when it emerges from the oven). Mark the biscuits into fingers or squares while still warm, but leave in the tin until completely cold. Don't make the biscuits too big – they are chewy and very filling.

Goosnargh Shortbread Biscuits

For a small village in Lancashire, Goosnargh seems to have developed more than its fair share of recipes, some of which appear in 'The Starter' and 'The Main Course' chapters.

Shortbread/cake tends to be associated with Scotland, but different forms of the biscuit have been made elsewhere in Britain, and regional varieties have their own distinctions. What makes Goosnargh cakes different is that they are flavoured with ground coriander and caraway seeds.

Makes about twenty biscuits
225g/8oz unsalted butter
125g/4½oz golden caster sugar (plus more for putting over biscuits)
350g/12oz plain flour
½ teaspoon ground coriander seeds
1½ teaspoons caraway seeds

Pre-heat oven to 180°C (355°F). Grease two baking sheets. Cream together butter and sugar until light and fluffy. Sift flour over the creamed mix, add the coriander and caraway seeds, mix with a wooden spoon until mixture resembles breadcrumbs. Using your hand, work mixture together to form a smooth paste. Take out of bowl and put onto a floured surface and knead gently so that dough is smooth and ready to roll out. Roll out and, using a circular cutter, cut out circular discs of dough. Place the discs onto the baking sheets, and sprinkle with caster sugar. Put the baking sheets into your fridge and leave for 30–60 minutes until well chilled. Place into the oven and bake for 15–20 minutes until just turned golden-brown. Remove from oven and sprinkle with more caster sugar. Leave to cool slightly then transfer to a wire rack.

NB: The 'short' in shortcake or shortbread, refers to the use of 'shortening' (butter or lard) in the mixture, which gives a soft, crumbling texture to the end product, but with a certain 'snap' – think how a finger of shortbread can be broken up so satfisfyingly into smaller lengths to pop in the mouth. Historically, shortcake and shortbread were one and the same – a form of sweetened pastry (flour, sugar, butter, water) rolled out, cut into shapes, and baked as biscuits.

English Oatmeal Digestives

Can any chapter of this nature be complete without a recipe for the traditional digestive biscuit? Café owner Tasmin Tate has updated this old recipe by introducing wholemeal flour and oatmeal, which she claims 'gives it a good nutty flavour.' She did, however, fail to comment on whether or not it made a good dunking biscuit!

110g/4oz wholemeal flour
110g/4oz oatmeal
10g/½oz Demerara sugar
75g/3oz butter
15ml/½fl oz milk
squeeze of lemon juice
pinch salt
½ teaspoon bicarbonate of soda

Place the flour, sugar, oatmeal, bicarbonate of soda, salt and lemon juice into a large bowl. Rub in the butter until the mixture resembles breadcrumbs. Add the milk and mix with a fork until it becomes manageable dough. Put it onto a large floured board and roll out to about 3mm thick. Cut out rounds with a pastry or biscuit cutter and prick all over the biscuit surface with a fork. Transfer to a greased baking tray and cook at 180°C (355°F) for about 15 minutes or until just very slightly browned. Lay out on a rack to cool.

Cornish Fairings

During the week after Christmas, a well attended 'hiring' fair used to be held at Launceston in Cornwall, and it was customary to eat or take home ginger-flavoured Fairings. Originally made with breadcrumbs, today's Cornish Fairings are made with plain flour.

Makes about two dozen
100g/3½oz plain flour
50g/2oz soft margarine
50g/2oz caster sugar
2 tablespoons golden syrup
½ teaspoon bicarbonate of soda
¼ teaspoon each ground ginger, mixed spice and ground cinnamon

Put the flour, spices and bicarbonate of soda into a bowl and rub in the margarine until the mixture is that of fine breadcrumbs. Mix in the sugar; gently melt the syrup and stir it into the mixture until a fine dough is formed. Roll into balls about the size of a cherry and place on two lightly greased baking trays before baking for 10 minutes at 180°C (355°F). Take the trays from the oven and hit them firmly on a solid surface to make the biscuit mixture crack and spread. Bake for a further 5 minutes and then place out to cool on a wire rack.

Jane's Biscuits for Cheese

It's often difficult to decide what best accompanies a good British cheese. Sometimes fruit is perfect or even a slice or two of freshly baked bread, but these simple biscuits go extremely well with most soft and creamy types of cheese. We've no idea who the 'Jane' was/is who gave her name to these particular biscuits as the hand-written copy of this recipe was discovered in the pages of a second-hand cookery book!

225g/8oz plain unbleached flour
25g/1oz butter
150ml/5fl oz hot milk
pinch of salt

Put the flour and salt into a large bowl and rub in the butter. Slowly pour in the hot milk, mixing as you go to make a firm, soft dough (you may need to add more or less milk according to how absorbent the flour is). Put the dough on a board and knead it well. Cut into six lumps and roll each out very thinly (which, according to 'Jane', is 'very hard work'). When it is paper-thin, cut out circles 4cm (1½in) in diameter and put onto a greased baking tray. Bake at 220°C (430°F) for 5 minutes until puffy and slightly browned in places. As with all biscuits, cool on a wire rack.

Chutneys, Pickles and Sauces

Despite now being associated with traditional and regional UK foods, especially cold meats and, latterly, the ubiquitous pub Ploughman's, chutneys actually originated in India and were first mentioned in British cooking books in the 1600s. The name is a derivation of the word 'Chatni', which was used to describe a strong, sweet relish. Pickling has been used since at least Roman times as a means of preserving fruit and vegetables at times of a glut. Strong-tasting sauces were thought to have developed as a means of disguising the taste of meat and fish that was, shall we say, 'past its best', but have since been turned into an art form where the delicate nuances of taste enhanced rather than hid the flavour of high-quality main course ingredients.

To make the best chutneys, pickles and relishes, it is necessary to choose fruit and vegetables that are fresh and totally free of rot or blemishes. Cook them slowly as the recipes dictate, in order to impart the dark colour and rich, gentle taste so typical of a good chutney or pickle. Generally, chutneys will improve in taste and texture by being kept for a couple of months before use, although, as can be seen from a few of the following recipes, some are ready to eat almost as soon as they are made. If you have a traditional larder, they are undoubtedly the best places in which to store any chutneys, pickles and relishes.

Many pickles and chutneys are regional in origin.

~ CHUTNEYS ~

West Country Pear Chutney

Perfect with a good chunk of mature Cheddar cheese as part of a Ploughman's lunch. It will keep for two to three months in the larder and, in fact, storing will intensify and improve the flavour.

Makes about five jars
2kg/4½lb pears, peeled, cored and roughly chopped
1kg/2½lb onions, finely chopped
1 clove of garlic
600ml/1pt cider vinegar
350g/12oz caster sugar
sachet of pickling spice (or 25g/1oz of same, tied tightly into a small piece of muslin)
2 teaspoons turmeric
25g/1oz cornflour

Place the pears, onions, garlic, cider vinegar and pickling spice into a heavy-bottomed (or preserving) pan and cook over a low heat, stirring gently so as to ensure that no ingredients stick. Once the pears have formed a purée and the onions have softened, stir in the sugar until it has dissolved. Taste the mixture and add more sugar if too tart for your liking. Bring to the boil and then simmer for 5 minutes before spooning out and throwing away the sachet/bag of pickling spice. Mix the turmeric and the cornflour with a little water to make a paste and add to the chutney. Bring to the boil, stirring until it thickens even more (if the chutney appears runnier than desired at the point of removing the pickling spices, double the quantity of cornflour added to the turmeric). Spoon into five clean, sterilized, normal-sized jam jars; sealing the lids whilst the chutney is still hot.

NB: When making any sort of chutney, always use stainless steel or enamelled pans because vinegar eats into those made of iron, copper, or brass.

Elderberry Chutney

Apart from perhaps blackberries, there can be nothing more traditional and best suited to a book on country cooking than elderberries. As with the majority of chutneys, this particular recipe tastes better if you allow it to mature for a few weeks before eating it.

Makes about 1.75kg (4lb)
450g/1lb elderberries
1.25kg/2¾lb apples
100g/3½oz stoned prunes
50g/2oz sultanas
50g/2oz chopped stem ginger
900ml/1½pt white wine vinegar
550g/1¼lb dark brown sugar
2 teaspoons ground all-spice
90ml/3fl oz ginger wine

Remove the elderberries from their stems, wash them lightly and dry well. Peel and core the apples and chop them into medium chunks. Chop the prunes into small chunks. Place all the ingredients into a large heavy-bottomed pan and cook until the sugar has dissolved. Bring the mixture to the boil and then simmer for 1 hour, stirring occasionally, until it has thickened.

Have some warm, well-cleaned jam jars waiting and pour or ladle the mixture into them. Seal at once with cellophane lids or clean, non-metallic screw tops.

NB: To test whether any type of chutney is cooked, make a 'channel' across the surface in the pan with a wooden spoon – if the impression lasts for a few seconds and does not fill up with liquid, then the chutney is ready to bottle.

A selection of autumnal chutneys and pickles.

Goosnargh Orange and Lemon Chutney

The little village of Goosnargh has no end to its culinary talents! As well as those found in the 'Starters' and 'Main Course' chapters of this book, this local recipe for Orange and Lemon chutney accompanies the duck of the region and goes well with goose and cold ham slices.

2 oranges, washed and scrubbed
3 lemons, washed and scrubbed
450g/1lb cooking apples
450g/1lb sugar
450ml/16fl oz white wine vinegar
225g/8oz onions, finely chopped
175g/6oz sultanas
1 blade mace
1 cinnamon stick
1 piece fresh root ginger, roughly scraped
1 teaspoon whole cloves
a few peppercorns
salt and pepper

Halve the oranges and lemons and squeeze their juices into a bowl. Finely shred the peel and flesh (carefully discarding the pips). Add the peel and flesh to the bowl containing the juice and add the vinegar and all the spices. Mix together well and leave to stand for at least a day. Place the mixture into a large chutney pan; peel, core and chop the apples and add to the pan, together with the onions. Cook very gently over a low heat until the fruit and onions are tender. Remove the pan from the heat before stirring in the sultanas, sugar and a little salt and pepper to taste. Stir in and, once the sugar appears to have dissolved, return to the heat and bring the contents of the pan to the boil. Reduce the heat and simmer gently for approximately 1 hour, or until the mixture is thick and all the juices absorbed. As with almost all chutneys, pour into warm, sterilized jars and seal immediately.

Beatrice Laval's Lavender Chutney

One of the authors lives in France and this recipe was given to him by a French neighbour. Technically, therefore, outside the scope of a book containing only country recipes from the regions of Britain; it is, having tasted it, too good not to include in this particular section! Beatrice uses it as an accompaniment to French cheese, with which it 'marries' very well.

20 lavender flowers, chopped into small pieces
3 lemons, washed and roughly chopped
3 onions, finely chopped
75g/3oz sultanas
white wine vinegar (enough to cover the chopped lemons)
2 tablespoons mustard seeds
1 cinnamon stick
pinch of ground all-spice
salt to taste
sugar to taste

Remove the pips and pith from the lemons and, in a bowl, cover them with vinegar before leaving to stand overnight. Place the lemons and vinegar into a pan and add the remainder of the ingredients. Stir until the sugar has dissolved and then bring the pan and its contents to the boil before reducing the heat and simmering gently until the mixture thickens. Remove the cinnamon stick before spooning or pouring into warmed storage jars and sealing tightly.

Crab Apple Chutney

Crab apples can be found throughout the British countryside and they make a simple to prepare chutney that is a very good accompaniment to all manner of cold meats. Perhaps it may be necessary to adjust the sugar quantities – depending on how 'sharp' you like your chutney.

2.25kg/5lb apples, peeled and cored
225g/8oz dates, stoned
115g/4oz raisins and/or sultanas
225g/8oz onions, minced
6 chillies
450g/1lb Demerara sugar
600ml/1pt vinegar
1 tablespoon salt
1 tablespoon powdered ginger

Place all the ingredients, together with a little of the vinegar, in a pan, bring to the boil, and add more vinegar as required until all is absorbed. Stir well until the fruit is soft and the mixture is of a thick consistency. Place in clean warm jars, cool, seal and store.

Red Tomato Chutney

It is often possible to find locally grown tomatoes at farmers' markets, sometimes by the tray-load and quite cheaply during late summer when there is a 'glut'. As well as using them fresh in cooking, and as the main ingredient in soups, which can then be frozen, they produce superb chutney, which can be used as an accompaniment to all manner of meals. This traditional recipe has been given an additional 'twist' by Beryl Woodhouse (*see* also: *Onion Relish*), who uses a bouquet garni rather than relying entirely on shop-bought pickling spices.

1kg/2¼lb ripe tomatoes, skinned and roughly chopped
2 onions, peeled and finely chopped
1 cooking apple, peeled, cored and finely chopped
175g/6oz seedless raisins
2 cloves garlic, peeled and crushed
14g/½oz fresh ginger, scraped and crushed
60g/2oz brown sugar
300ml/10fl oz vinegar
bouquet garni, made up of 1 crushed bay leaf, 4–5 cloves,
2–3 crushed dried chillies; ½ teaspoon mustard seeds,
plus a few each of cardamoms, cinnamon, coriander and peppercorns

Simmer the chopped onions in a large saucepan with a little water before adding the apple and raisins and cooking gently until they soften. Add the tomatoes, garlic, ginger and sugar, and mix together thoroughly before including the vinegar and bouquet garni. Cook on a low heat for about 1 hour, or until the mixture has thickened so much that when a groove is made across the surface in the pan with a wooden spoon the impression lasts for a few seconds and does not fill up with liquid. Finally, spoon into hot, clean jars and seal immediately.

Kent Windfall Chutney

As a gardener, there always seems to be more unripe green tomatoes left at the end of the growing season than one knows what to do with! It's always possible to make traditional green tomato chutney, but blending them with windfall plums, pears and apples to produce a chutney that works well with either cold meats or strong regional cheeses is, in our opinion, a far better idea!

Makes about 4kg of chutney
1kg/2¼lb apples, peeled, cored and chopped into chunks of about 1.5cm (½in)
1kg/2¼lb pears, peeled, cored and chopped the same as the apples
1kg/2¼lb plums, stoned
900g/2lb onions, peeled and chopped
900g/2lb green tomatoes, washed and quartered
225g/8oz mixed seedless raisins and sultanas
450g/1lb marrow flesh, cut into small cubes
850ml/1½pt malt vinegar
50g/2oz pickling spice (in sachets or tied into a corner of muslin to form a bouquet garni)
225g/8oz soft brown sugar
50g/2oz salt

Place the fruit, tomatoes, raisins and sultanas, marrow and onions into a large pan. Add half the amount of vinegar and the spices before bringing to the boil. Simmer until the ingredients are tender and pulpy in texture; stir occasionally. Add the sugar, salt and remainder of the vinegar, stirring continuously until the sugar has completely dissolved. Continue cooking over a low heat, giving the chutney an occasional stir from time to time until the mixture becomes thick – this may take up to 2 hours. Once cooked, remove the spice bag(s), spoon into clean, sterilized jars and seal. Store for at least a month before using.

NB: When using windfalls, be sure to cut out any obviously bruised sections and use only that which is sound – for that reason, it may pay to increase the weights of windfalls given in the recipe to be sure of ending up with the correct amount of prepared fruit.

Clod Hall Chutney

Carola Morrison runs a very successful bed and breakfast at Clod Hall, Milson, Cleobury Mortimer, Shropshire, and included this recipe in a 'Recipe Calendar' compiled and produced on behalf of the South Shropshire Farm Holiday Group. She was kind enough to also allow us to use it here. Carola says that 'chutney can be added to stews for extra piquancy.'

Makes about 1.5kg/3⅓lb
1.35kg/3lb cooking apples
2 large onions
900ml/1½pt malt vinegar
900g/2lb brown sugar
450g/1lb chopped raisins
250g/9oz crystallized ginger, chopped
2 tablespoons turmeric
1 teaspoon salt
2 teaspoons dry mustard
½ teaspoon cayenne pepper

Peel, core and chop the apples and onions. Add the vinegar, boil to a pulp. Add the other ingredients and mix in well. Boil again for a further 30 minutes, stirring often. Ladle into jars and cover.

Onion Relish

Beryl Woodhouse, of Staffordshire – one of our kindly hosts as we ate (sorry, photographed) our way around Britain, gave us this recipe for an onion-lover's relish, saying that 'it should be stored in the fridge and will keep for about a month.'

Serves eight
675g/1½lb onions
125g/4½oz butter
175g/6oz sugar
225ml/8oz red wine
100ml/3½fl oz red wine vinegar
salt and pepper

Peel and slice the onions thinly. Heat the butter in a pan and, once it has melted, cook it for 1–2 minutes without letting it brown and burn. Add the onions and a little seasoning. Stir in the sugar and mix well before simmering for 30–35 minutes with the pan lid covering. Stir in the vinegar and red wine and cook for another 30 minutes, this time with the lid off. Stir frequently at this stage and when thickened, ladle into warmed, sterilized jars and cover immediately.

~ PICKLES ~

Spiced Pineapple Pickle

To be served with *Pressed Terrine of Yorkshire Gammon with Fried Ledstone Quail Egg, Spiced Pineapple Pickle, Mustard Seed Dressing* (see page 45).

1 pineapple, skinned cored and finely chopped
1 clove garlic, crushed
1 teaspoon grain mustard
3 tablespoons white wine vinegar
pinch saffron strands
150g Demerara sugar
pinch of salt

Place all the ingredients into a heavy-bottomed pan; stir in a pinch of salt and simmer gently for about 1½ hours, until a golden yellow colour. When at the right consistency, spoon into an airtight jar. Leave to cool before sealing the jar. This can be made in advance and will keep for 3–4 weeks.

Onions are a basic ingredient of many pickles and chutneys – red onions generally make a sweeter alternative to white or 'Spanish'.

Pickled Worcester Plums

Writing a book of this nature is a delight, not only because of the recipes learned and used, but also because of the kind, enthusiastic people we met during its compilation. Our September trip involved a stay at Sally Olstead's bed and breakfast and, once she knew the purpose of our visit, offered the following recipe, which apparently was frequently made by her mother-in-law. Sally says that this particular pickle is 'just right for eating with any cold meat, but I remember it best when it was used by my mother-in-law alongside one of her own, very special cold game pies, which she made after my father-in-law's various shooting expeditions.'

450g/1lb plums, washed, dried and de-stalked
rind of half a lemon
225g/8oz sugar
300ml/10fl oz white vinegar
small piece fresh root ginger, bruised
4 whole cloves
1 cinnamon stick

Prick the plums all over with a fork before placing them in a pan. Add the vinegar and sugar. Make a bouquet garni of the lemon rind and spices by tying them tightly into a small square of muslin and add this to the pan also. Heat gently, stirring all the time until the plums are tender (but do not leave them so long that the skins split). Gently remove the plums from the liquid mixture with a perforated spoon and place into storage jars. Remove the bouquet garni before boiling the liquid rapidly for 5 minutes more. Pour over the plums and immediately seal the jars. For the best-tasting pickled Worcester plums, store in a cool, dark place for at least a month before using.

Red Cabbage Pickle

This traditional pickle is known in almost all of Britain's regions – probably due to its suitability as an accompaniment to cold meats and some hard cheeses.

2 red cabbages
100g/3½oz salt
600ml/1pt red wine vinegar
600ml/1pt distilled malt vinegar
4 bay leaves
4 whole dried chillies
1 tablespoon juniper berries
1 tablespoon black peppercorns
1 dessertspoon coriander seeds
small piece fresh ginger

Quarter the cabbages and remove stem and core. Shred very finely and place in a bowl, sprinkling layers with salt, and leave for 24 hours. Meanwhile, put the vinegars into a pan and add all the spices with the exception of the bay leaves and juniper. Bring to the boil and then simmer for 5 minutes before placing to one side to cool. Next day wash and drain cabbage and pack into four jars with bay leaves and juniper berries. Pour in the strained vinegar and tightly seal the lids.

NB: For any chutney or pickle, always use plastic-lined lids, as vinegar very quickly eats into metal lids.

Pickled Marsh Samphire

Samphire can be used raw in salads, though it tends to be a little salty so try boiling or steaming it first. You won't find many recipes that use samphire, but we have included a few ideas in both this chapter and in that dealing with main courses. As it is very seasonal, growing only in late July/August, and it does not freeze well, to be able to use it at any other times (and this does, we must admit, go against much of what we advocate throughout this book, whereby things should only be enjoyed 'in season'), it will be neccesary to pickle some.

Makes roughly three large jars
1.35kg/3¼lb wild samphire shoots
12 garlic cloves, peeled and scored
850ml/1½pt water
850ml/1½pt white vinegar
350g/12oz sugar
3 level tablespoons pickling spice

Prepare the samphire by removing the tender shoots from any of the more woody stems. Soak the shoots in cold water for 1 hour and finally rinse off by placing them in a colander and flushing them under cold running water. Chop into short, 5cm (2in) lengths.

Prepare the storage jars by sterilizing them (baby bottle cleaning tablets are good for this job) and into each place four of the garlic cloves and a tablespoon of pickling spice. Add the lengths of samphire until each jar is full.

Put the remainder of the ingredients into a pan and bring it to the boil before allowing it to simmer for approximately 15 minutes. Then pour the liquid over the samphire, spices and cloves (making sure to leave a little air-space at the top of each jar). Seal whilst still hot and stand the jars in a bowl of just-boiling water for 15 minutes, but make sure that the liquid and the water is not so hot that you run the risk of cracking the glass of the jars. The pickled samphire can be eaten after about a week; however, the longer it is stored, the more flavoursome it will become.

~ SAUCES ~

Yorkshire Sauce

My grandmother used to make this when I was young – I hated it! Reintroduced to it recently in connection with this book, I love it! It goes well with cold, locally produced cold meats.

1ltr/2pt malt vinegar
2 × 50g/2oz tins anchovies (drained and patted dry with kitchen paper)
4 cloves garlic, peeled and chopped
4 shallots, peeled and chopped
1 tablespoon brown sugar
3 tablespoons dark soy sauce
1 teaspoon ground mace
1 teaspoon cayenne pepper
½ teaspoon ground all-spice

Blend all the ingredients, with the exception of vinegar, in a food processor. Place into large jars, add the vinegar and cover. Shake every day for a month. Strain through muslin and bottle.

Coln Valley Gooseberry Sauce

The original of this simple recipe dates from the 1700s, when it was popular for use with fish such as mackerel. Cotswold river fishermen have since modified it into something which is delicious when accompanying freshly caught trout – the sharpness of the gooseberries giving a good contrasting flavour to the mild-tasting flesh of the fish.

350g/12oz gooseberries, washed and topped and tailed
25g/1oz butter
25g/1oz sugar
300ml/10fl oz water
½ level teaspoon ground nutmeg
pinch of salt and black pepper

Boil the gooseberries in the water for about 5 minutes. Purée – either in a liquidizer or by pushing through a sieve – before returning to the pan. Add the rest of the ingredients and reheat until all the sugar is dissolved, but do not allow it to boil.

Cumberland Sauce

This sauce finds its way into a book dealing with regional recipes by default, as the name actually refers to its connection with one of the Dukes of Cumberland rather than it originating from Cumbria. No matter, it makes a good base for things like game casserole, is a perfect substitute for chutney in sandwiches and makes a tasty accompaniment to cold meats. It will keep for weeks in the larder or months in the fridge.

3 large oranges
3 lemons
175g/6oz onions, finely chopped
350g/12oz redcurrant jelly
2 teaspoons English mustard, made-up, not still in powder form
50ml/2fl oz cider vinegar
a pinch each ground mace, ground ginger and salt
1 tablespoon cooking oil

Grate the peel from the oranges and lemons. Squeeze the juice onto a bowl and mix the peel into that before leaving it to stand for at least 30 minutes. Meanwhile, cook the onions in the oil for about 10 minutes (they should be clean and soft, not brown and burnt!). Add the redcurrant jelly, the orange and lemon mixture and stir in the mustard, vinegar, spices and salt. Simmer on a low heat until the jelly is completely dissolved and then boil for a further 5–10 minutes until the sauce begins obviously to thicken. Set aside to cool before 'bottling' and sealing in clean, sterilized jars.

Cullybackey Seafood Sauce

Jenny Bristow, cookery writer, radio and television presenter, lives with her family on their farm near the County Antrim village of Cullybackey. Jenny apparently often uses this particular recipe in place of a more conventional hollandaise sauce.

Serves ten/twelve
4 egg yolks
115–170g/4–6oz peeled prawns
225g/8oz melted butter
1 tablespoon tarragon vinegar
1 tablespoon lemon juice
2–3 dessertspoons whipped cream
1 teaspoon caster sugar
a few pink peppercorns
a few drops Tabasco sauce

Whisk the eggs and sugar over a pan of warm water for 2–3 minutes until slightly creamy. Transfer to a blender or food processor and whisk for 30 seconds. Slowly trickle in the vinegar and lemon juice while they are both warm, whisking occasionally. Finally add the melted butter (as slowly as possible, otherwise the sauce will end up being too thin). Transfer to a bowl, and then add the whipped cream, peeled prawns, peppercorns, and a few drops of Tabasco sauce.

Medway Medium Mustard Sauce

Mustard is an ancient herb and, like most things, was introduced to Britain by the Romans, who used it to preserve the freshness of meat and fish. Mustard is the best friend of pork and, whilst it's possible to buy it ready prepared, nothing beats a sauce that has been freshly prepared at home. This particular recipe was found hand-written and tucked into a recipe book bought at a garden fete in Kent. Quantities are therefore presented exactly as written and have been tried and tested by the authors! (1 cup is equivalent to 250ml.)

Makes two cups
4 tablespoons butter
4 tablespoons flour
1–2 tablespoons dry mustard
1 teaspoon sugar
2 cups beef bouillon (beef stock)

Melt the butter in a saucepan over low heat. Add flour, mustard and sugar; stir until smooth. Slowly add the bouillon, stirring constantly to avoid lumps. Cook, stirring until smooth and thickened. For a very thick sauce, increase the flour to half a cup.

Swindlebury Sweet Game Sauce

It is traditional to serve sweet sauces with game. This one is slightly unusual in the fact that it equally complements any cold meat and is also perfect when used as a topping for ice-cream – yes, really!

175g/6oz butter
40g/1½oz pistachio nuts, roughly chopped
115g/4oz soft brown sugar
60ml/2fl oz dark rum
60ml/2fl oz brandy
1 teaspoon freshly grated ginger
½ teaspoon nutmeg

Melt the butter in a heavy-bottomed saucepan. Add the spices, nuts and sugar before heating for about 1 minute. Gradually stir in the alcohol and simmer over a very low heat until all the ingredients have combined. Pour into a sauceboat and serve straight away.

Creamed Apple Sauce

We included this recipe from a Devon gamekeeper's wife in our book *Cook Game* (Crowood Press, 2008) because it goes very well with all manner of game, wildfowl and wild boar. As with many sauces, it uses alcohol, but it is important to remember that the idea of adding alcohol to sauces is not to get your guests 'sloshed' in double-quick time, but to enhance whatever you are serving by adding a subtle flavour.

115g/4oz butter
2 eating apples, peeled, cored and sliced
250ml/8fl oz game stock (made-up chicken cubes or granules will suffice)
2 tablespoons fresh tarragon, finely chopped
250ml/8fl oz cider
125ml/4fl oz white dessert wine
60ml/2fl oz apple brandy
125ml/4fl oz double cream

Melt the butter in a pan before adding the apple slices. Once these have softened, add the game stock together with the tarragon. Simmer over a low heat for a couple of minutes and slowly begin including the alcohol. When all is gently simmering, finally stir in the cream and serve immediately.

Sauces make a good accompaniment to many dishes – in particular, those involving fish.

Wild Samphire Sauce

Sheila Benson and Sean Millar, cookery writers for the *Liverpool Daily Post*, are keen to extall the virtues of wild samphire grass, otherwise known as salicorn or 'sea asparagus'. Samphire is a type of marsh grass that grows naturally on sea inlets. It lives off nutrients from the sea and produces robust, green stalks similar to baby asparagus, hence the name.

It's an unusual ingredient, but it works so well as an accompaniment to fish, shellfish and lamb. Keen as the authors are on local, regional and seasonal ingredients, it may be useful to point out that August is the best month to find it growing wild. If obtainable, it is well worth considering for use in fish dishes or, as here, in a sauce to accompany cold salmon and trout.

2–3 handfuls young samphire fronds
zest and juice of a lemon
30ml/1fl oz olive oil
250ml/8fl oz crème fraîche
salt and ground black pepper to season

In a colander, rinse the samphire under cold running water. Chop roughly and purée in a food processor before slowly adding the olive oil and seasoning. Transfer the purée to a mixing bowl and gently fold in the crème fraîche, zest and lemon juice to taste.

Cheese and Wine

Cheese and wine have always been connected with each other – well, at least since the sometimes 'tacky' days of the 1970s when, along with fondue parties and kaftan dresses, cheese and wine parties were an essential of 'civilized' entertaining. Why such a combination should ever have been considered is open to speculation, as it is well-known that cheese masks the subtle flavour of a good wine.

Some years ago, researchers asked a team of wine tasters to evaluate cheap and expensive versions of four different red wines, grading them on characteristic aromas such as oak, chocolate, dried fruit, mushroom and astringency. The tasters then assessed the wines again after eating a variety of cheeses, and proved without doubt that cheese dampens down the aromatic fruits, oaks and astringency of red wine. They found that only wines with a 'buttery' aroma were enhanced by cheese – probably because cheese itself contains diacetyl, the molecule responsible for a buttery wine aroma. Strong cheeses undoubtedly suppressed flavour more than the milder cheeses, but the nuances of *all* the wines were more difficult to detect. It is obvious from what the tasters noted that the marriage of cheese and wine isn't as simple as it sounds, but although some pairings can be a disaster, something like a really good mature Cheddar and a young wine made from the cabernet sauvignon-type grape is, in our humble opinion, a wonderful combination.

~ CHEESE ~

Since the Norman Conquest in 1066, cheese has played an important role in the British economy and diet. Most regions developed their own cheeses, but unlike the rest of Europe, the majority of these traditional cheeses were almost exclusively hard or blue. Recently, however, there has been an enormous interest in cheese making – resulting in a rich diversity of over 450 unique modern and traditional types. Old recipes have been revived and new ones developed using old methods, recipes and milk from rare breeds of animals. Therefore, no trip around Britain in search of traditional and regional recipes that have been given a 'lift' by some enterprising chefs, restaurateurs, cooks, local producers and growers can be considered complete without at least mentioning some of the exciting cheeses being made throughout the country. No longer is it necessary to just pick up a piece of Wensleydale, Lancashire, Cheshire, Cheddar or Red Leicester (although you can of course do so should you so wish), nor is it necessary to make do with cheese that is as yellow and rubbery as a bathroom duck. Britain has, over the past decade or so, become a country of exciting cheeses, a plate of which will enhance the end of any meal. Alternativaly it can be served, as the French do, between the main course and the pudding.

Just a few examples of traditional regional cheeses.

uliar Swaledale.
d has been soaked in
Old Peculier Yorkshire Ale.

0gms **£2·00**
100g

WENSLEYDALE WITH APRICOT.
**Mild and crumbly Wensleydale
containing small pieces of apricot.
Light and refreshing.**
£ **1.25** er 100 gms

WHAT GOES WITH WHAT

Wine can be a problem when combined with cheese and there is no doubt that what you eat and drink with cheese will either deaden or improve its flavour to your taste buds. Celery, grapes, or even, as seen on the French dinner table, lettuce, will add to the subtle flavours of most. Radishes add peppery heat and colour while half a red or green dessert apple, sliced, is a well-known accompaniment. Pears are wonderful with Stilton – but they must be ripe; figs and prunes go well with goat's cheese, and dried apricots, passion fruit, cranberries, sliced melon, cherries and strawberries really enhance the taste of almost everything. The traditional hard cheeses of the Midlands go well with a glass of port and any hard cheese makes a good 'Ploughman's lunch' if served with pickles or a pickled onion or two. Be careful though with the latter: a vegetable-based sweet pickle is often better than a pickled onion, which tends to overwhelm the cheese with its vinegar flavour. Chutneys are a great accessory: try a roasted apple, gooseberry or simple fresh grape. A home-made 'marmalade' such as red onion works well and is simple to produce.

Red Onion Marmalade

2 red onions, thinly sliced
2 dessertspoons brown sugar
100ml/3½fl oz balsamic vinegar
1 tablespoon oil

Place the onions in a pan with the oil and cook gently until the onions have softened. Add the sugar and vinegar, cooking slowly for a further 10 minutes. Allow to cool before serving. This 'marmalade' will keep for months if stored in a cool place.

SOURCING, BUYING AND STORING CHEESE

Most artisan cheese-makers sell organic cheese made from organic milk, so they offer all the environmental, humanitarian and healthy eating benefits of other organic dairy products. Buying organic is a 'must' if you want to avoid the possibility of eating genetically modified rennet. If possible, buy pieces of hard and semi-hard cheese cut fresh from the whole cheese because that which is ready-cut is likely to go stale quicker. Do not buy cheese that has cracks running from the edges, or is darker in the middle than it is on the outside: it is stale and in the process of drying out. Likewise, avoid cheese that is 'sweating', as it is a sure sign that it has been previously stored at too high a temperature and, as a result, the flavour may well be impaired. Semi-soft cheeses, such as brie, that have a 'chalky' layer running through the middle are not ripe and will taste dry and tangy – do not take it home in the fond hope that it will improve with keeping – the very complicated process of 'ripening' is best done by the producer and is unlikely to be replicated by yourself.

Farmers' markets are one of the best places to source regional cheeses.

To get the best from any cheese, it needs to be carefully kept and served. Debbie Bell, who has a stall on Easingwold market in Yorkshire, feels that 'cheese should be kept in greaseproof paper and kept in the salad drawer of the fridge before being brought out 2 hours before you need it. If you have a larder; then that's the best place to keep cheeses like mature Cheddar. Generally, light destroys the B vitamin, so keep it in the dark.'

Remember that some cheeses are seasonal, so the availability of some, particularly sheep's cheeses, are obviously dependent on lambing times and the subsequent lactation periods. Of the others, there is a plentiful choice, but it seems that from the producers we have spoken to, visitors to an area want to buy local types in order to experience the topography's unique tastes. Strangely however, locals also tend to buy 'local' too! Farmers' markets are the easiest place to source cheese, and each year the numbers of such markets increase. As Tracy Frankpitt of the Peverstone Cheese Company near Cullompton, Devon observes:

> We wanted to sell our award-winning cheese – Devon Garland, Tiskey Meadow and Hunting Pink – at the farmers' market in Bath but they said we were too far away. Cullompton was looking for something that would bring more people into the town and I suggested we started our own farmers' market. Which we did!

CHEESES FROM AROUND THE REGIONS

Draw a line down the centre of the UK. To the east you have grain and the big fields of East Anglia. To the west, you have dairy cows, milk and cheese. Artisan cheese-makers are nowadays either redeveloping long-lost regional cheeses or devising new ones based on traditional recipes. Much of the initial thinking behind this was that, not only were people beginning to realize the importance of 'lost' foods and, through various television chefs, the benefits of local producers, but also many began cheese making when dairy farming began to get into difficulties and, without some form of diversification, they would have found it very difficult to continue with their family-run farm. Their considerable 'portfolios' now includes a premium range of traditional, hand-made cheeses all of which are created by using locally sourced cow's, ewe's, goat's and even buffalo's milk.

THE WEST COUNTRY

The West Country has a wide variety of cheeses, the best-known of which must be Cheddar in all its different guises. Blue Vinney is a hard, white, blue-veined cheese originating from Dorset. Also from the region are Curworthy, Devon Garland, and Cornish Yarg, distinctive with its nettle rind (the name sounds Cornish, but is, in fact, the maker's name, Gray, spelt backwards!). Made in the heart of Somerset, Wessex Goat Cheese has a lovely full flavour – despite it being a young cheese; Tymsboro, produced on a farm near Bath, is a goat's cheese described as having the taste of 'lemon sorbet and apples' and is usually presented in the shape of a flat-topped pyramid and the natural rind, dusted with black ash, is covered with a white mould. If you're searching for something really different, there is the Beenleigh Blue, which is made from the milk of sheep grazed on Dartmoor. Like many speciality cheeses, it is seasonal and comes into its best for the autumn and winter. Another ewe's milk cheese is Sheviok, which comes from Cornwall. For a brie-style, look out for Sharpham Full Fat Soft Cheese produced from a herd of Jersey cows that feeds in the meadows alongside the river Dart.

WALES, SHROPSHIRE, GLOUCESTER, HEREFORDSHIRE AND ELSEWHERE!

If you want a really local cheese, try 'Finn'. Hand-made in the village of Dorstone, Herefordshire, by Charlie Westhead, it is apparently named after his dog! More conventionally, whilst travelling in connection with this book, we were regularly finding Hereford Hop, a hard pasteurized cheese wrapped in hops: the hops are crunchy, with the slightly yeasty taste associated with beer, while the cheese is mellow, sweet and buttery. Also produced in Dorstone is the hand-made Ragstone – a medium-fat matured cheese derived from unpasteurized goat's milk. Shropshire Blue has its followers and, moving into Wales, there is the Y-Fenni, produced with the addition of parsley and mustard seeds. In the heart of west Wales can be found Golden Cenarth, made by Gwynfor and Thelma Adams who established their cheese-making business in 1987 as a response to the EU milk quotas that had threatened the viability of the family farm. Snowdonia lends its name to the rather alarming sounding 'Green Thunder' and 'Black Bomber' varieties. Also to be found locally in the regions of Wales are Llangloffan; Pencarreg Brie; Caws Fferm Teifi (an aged Gouda-style); and Llanboidy, made from the milk of the Red Poll cattle. Caerphilly is, however, probably the best known of all Welsh cheeses. Travelling back into Gloucestershire, there is not only the obvious choice between Single and Double, but also the delightful-sounding Birdwood Blue Heaven. This mould-ripened, soft blue cheese is made from unpasteurized, home-produced cow's milk. The bizarrely-named Stinking Bishop, made from the milk of the rare Gloucester cow, has found fame and fortune since becoming associated in the public's mind with the Wallace and Gromit animated film, *The Curse of the Were-Rabbit*. Smelling like a teenage boy's bedroom, it is, nevertheless, a mild, easy-eating cheese, producing a slightly nutty flavour, together with subtle fruity overtones – obtained by being rind-washed in perry. Wiltshire, although not a big cheese producer, nevertheless produces Wigmore, Waterloo and, stretching the county boundaries even further, there is the ammonite-shaped Barkham Blue from Berkshire.

THE MIDLANDS (AND KENT!)
As a result of the majority of milk being produced down the western and middle of Britain, it is not surprising to find so many different varieties of cheese originating from the Midlands. Well-known types include Cheshire, Red Leicester and, of course, Blue Stilton. Long Clawson Stilton has a delicious creamy texture and is made in a village outside Melton Mowbray. Lesser-known are Sage Derby and Coldwick – the latter traditionally sold at the famous Nottingham Goose Fair. Another variation on the Derby cheese is Fowler's Little Derby, perversely nowadays made in Warwickshire as result of the Fowler family moving from Derbyshire to Warwickshire in 1918 (they have been producing Derby cheese since 1840 – making them possibly the oldest cheese-making family anywhere in Britain). Is Oxfordshire in the Midlands? Well, wherever it is geographically, it's on the cheese-making map due to it producing True Bloo Ewe, an excellent blue made from sheep's milk. Similarly, as a result of Kent (yes, we know it's not in the Midlands!) being better known for its sheep than its cattle, it is not surprising that it produces little in the way of cheese – the county is, nevertheless, home to the producers of Crockhamdale, a hard, unpasteurized cheese possessing an interesting nutty flavour, which is made from ewe's milk.

YORKSHIRE AND LANCASHIRE
Yorkshire has a great selection of cheeses: the best-selling Yorkshire Blue, for instance, is a very creamy version of a Stilton type whilst 'Old Peculiar' Swaledale has the delightful addition of Theakson's Yorkshire Ale. Amongst others (many of which are produced by Judy Bell at Shepherds Pure Cheeses) are Mrs Bell's Blue, Buffalo Blue, Byland Blue, Old York, Basilano, Smoked Jersey, Coverdale, Cotherstone, Katy's White Lavender and Rydale. There is even a 'Fine Fettle Yorkshire Cheese', which is a feta-type but, because of EU regulations preventing anyone from calling a cheese 'feta' if it's not been made in the Feta region of Greece, cannot be called that! Across the Pennines in Lancashire is the crumbly, pale-coloured, buttery and slightly salty-tasting cheese of the same name. Head directly north-east into Northumberland and you will encounter Admiral Collingwood and Baltic, both with rinds washed in local ale. Others include Redesdale ewe's milk cheese.

There are some excellent cheeses coming from the rugged landscapes of Yorkshire . . .

. . . and Lancashire.

SCOTLAND AND IRELAND

From the very far north comes a soft goat's cheese, produced from a herd based on the Isle of Arran off the coast of Scotland. Again seasonal, it is available between April and November. The Highland cheese makers specialize in soft cheeses, of which Crowdie, said to have been introduced by the Vikings, is probably the best-known. Others include Caboc, a rich cream cheese rolled in oatmeal (similar in fact to Howgate); Lanark Blue – made from unpasteurized milk taken from ewes who graze the heather-covered hills of Strathclyde and available only from June to January; Dunlop and Langskaill. Across the water in Ireland there is the classic Irish Cheddar; Cashel Blue – the creamiest of blue cheeses; rich, strong, Camembert-style Cooleeney, made from unpasteurized cow's milk; and Coolea, a nutty, sweet Gouda-style cheese made from pasteurized cow's milk.

CHEESE ROLLING

If your love of cheese extends to not just eating it but also rolling it down a hill, then you can do no better than attending one of the events held annually in Gloucester. At Randwick, things kick off in a slightly more sedate fashion than they do at Cooper's Hill: after a Blessing, the cheeses – there are normally three of them – are taken for a genteel stroll (or should that be roll?) in an anti-clockwise direction around the local church, after which one of the cheeses is cut into pieces and shared amongst the onlookers. The other two cheeses are kept until the following weekend when they are paraded through the streets accompanied by a 'Mop Man' whose whole aim in life is to 'sweep' the crowds away with a wet mop. He is joined by a Flag Man, a Sword Bearer, two Cheese Bearers, a May Queen and the Mayor: the latter is eventually dipped in the Mayor's Pool – which begs the question as to whether there's any kudos in status. The procession then moves on to Well Leaze, where the cheeses are rolled and chased down the hillside by those mad enough to do so.

~ WINES ~

Changes in farming subsidies, and the warmer British summers of recent years, are persuading more and more farmers to diversify into wine production, with the result that there are now nearly 1,000 hectares given over to growing vines and an average of 2.5 million bottles produced each year. But wine production in the UK is no new thing. Some say that the Romans brought vines to the British Isles, but it is more likely that they brought flagons of wine rather than the plants from which to make it. Like cheese making, it is however, known that vine growing began seriously with the Norman invasions, after which time they could be found growing in secluded monastery gardens in southern England. At that time, there were thought to be at least forty vineyards in existence, but by 1534 this number had increased to 140 throughout England and Wales. The Church still owned over a third of them, the remainder being in the hands of the monarchy and private landowners. Vine growing and wine making continued in a very minor way right up until the twentieth century and it was not until the 1980s and '90s that the numbers of vineyards really increased and the production of wine was taken seriously.

While for years it was mainly enthusiastic amateurs who produced English wine, it is now part of an industry run by committed professional producers and Major General Sir Guy Salisbury-Jones is credited by most to have been at the forefront of commercial English wine production, and he planted his first vineyard at Hambledon, Hampshire in 1951. There are now around 400 vineyards spread across Britain, as far north as Durham. Many of our wines are now ranked highly in top wine circles – even picking up international prizes. Typically, English still wine is white, aromatic, delicate and fruity. Increasingly, however, red wines, rosé and champagne types are being produced to a very high standard (most of the UK's wines are white and the few reds that are available are generally made from red-fleshed grapes or ripened in poly-tunnels). At the end of May 2007, the two most widely planted grape varieties were, according to *Hugh Johnson's Pocket Wine Book 2008*, Chardonnay and Pinot Noir. They will, by Johnson's reckoning, account for 'getting on for 50 per cent of the vineyard area by 2008–9.'

Not the same thing at all, but keep an eye out for the growing range of English country wines, which are made not from grapes but apples, redcurrants, gooseberries elderflowers and berries and other old-fashioned ingredients – they are a little more sophisticated than Granny used to make and well worth seeking out.

An English vineyard.

IDENTIFYING TYPES OF WINE

Generically, one might call wine produced in the UK British or English, but that would be wrong because there is a very big difference between the two. Basically a British wine is, although made in Britain, actually produced from grape juice concentrates brought in from abroad, whereas an English wine must, by law, be produced from grapes grown in this country – in reality, from England and Wales – the vagrancies of weather in Scotland preclude it from being a serious contender in wine production.

In the early 1990s, a scheme was introduced whereby it was possible for UK wine growers to have their grapes and wines assessed in much the same way as the French had for years been producing wine classified as *Appellation Controleé* – a title that indicated to the buyer the type of grape, the region in which it was grown and, in some cases, even the actual vineyard itself. This allows the use of descriptions such as 'quality wines', which must be made from pure grape varieties grown in a certain geographical area, checked as to chemical content and passed by a tasting panel, and 'regional wines', which are then further designated by the actual name of the region in which they are produced. They go through a similar testing to 'quality wines', but as they can contain a certain proportion of hybrid grapes, growers of Seyval Blanc, for example, cannot apply for registration in the former category. 'Table wines' can be made from any approved grape variety and produced with little or no outside examination or intervention, and are, in the opinion of some, best avoided. Others may be labelled as a sparkling wine, but never, of course, as champagne. Champagne can, because of EU regulations, only ever be called that if it is actually produced in that region of France. It is possible, however, to legitimately claim that your wine is produced using 'champagne methods'. Interestingly, a few years ago, 'Nyetimber Classic Cuvee', produced in West Sussex, was named the best sparkling wine in the world outside the Champagne region in an international wine competition.

PROBLEMS WITH WINE PRODUCTION

England's vineyards may be further from the Equator than many others but the Gulf Stream helps to moderate the climate, so much so that UK-grown vines need no special protection in the winter. However, vines need a south-facing slope with well-drained soil in order to survive. Frost kills the buds, high winds break down the vines, and if there is not enough sun, the grapes will not ripen properly.

Regions with high rainfall bring their own problems: fungal diseases such as rot and mildew flourish in damp conditions; spraying is not always a viable option as organic viticulture is becoming ever more popular with producers and wine buyers alike (it is far easier to practise organic growing methods in a dry climate than it is a damp one). It is also important that the correct vine varieties are grown in appropriate soil conditions and that their growing is based on scientific know-how. A hybrid grape, for example (generally produced from a crossing of the European cultivated vine and the American wild vine), is sometimes a more viable proposition due to its increased disease resistance. Seyval Blanc is well known amongst UK wine growers and, of the 'pure-bred' varieties; Müller-Thurgau and the German Reichensteiner are also quite widely planted. Award-winning wine writer Janice Robinson, comments:

> [In Britain] almost all grape musts have to rely on added sugar to produce wine with a decent alcoholic strength and the natural grape acidity is usually notable. Such wines can make excellent bases for sparkling wines and there have been some truly refreshing dry whites which can even stand up to some barrel-aging.

WINE AROUND THE REGIONS

English white wines go well with Colchester oysters or Dover sole, but ideally, with their delicate and aromatic flavours, they are, in the opinion of most, best drunk on their own.

SURREY, WEST SUSSEX, HAMPSHIRE AND THE WEST COUNTRY

Denbies' vineyard situated in Dorking, Surrey is reckoned to be the largest in the UK and covers some 100 hectares. It is an impressive place and produces very good Riesling, sweet wines and some reds. Nyetimber in West Sussex must also be mentioned due to the fact that, as mentioned previously, it has the undoubted honour of its 'Classic Cuvee' being named as the best sparkling wine in the world outside the Champagne region. It is, at the time of writing, under new ownership and there are plans to build a new winery and launch a non-vintage wine.

Other local wines include those from Nutbourne, Bookers, Ridgeview, Warnham and Highdown. The Hidden Spring vineyard at Horsham can probably supply you with a bottle or two of their Sunset Rosé. At Beaulieu Abbey, Hampshire, the traditions of growing on a monastic site are maintained and it is well worth taking a look, especially if you happen to be visiting the nearby Beaulieu Motor Museum. Hampshire seems to have spawned more than its fair share of vineyards over the years, including Danebury, Northbrook Springs, Priors Dean and Wickham. On the Isle of Wight, the Adgestone vineyards grow their grapes on the chalky downs overlooking Sandown, whilst the Rosemary vineyard is the island's largest in terms of hectares. Not only is Beenleigh home to the Beenleigh Blue cheese, but this Devon-based producer also makes award-winning, oak-aged Cabernet/Merlot wines as do nearby Sharpham. Camel Valley in Cornwall have produced some very good wines, especially Cornwall Brut and a sparkling rosé.

EAST SUSSEX, KENT AND ESSEX

In East Sussex can be found the interestingly named Breaky Bottom vineyard – its wines are, according to wine expert Oz Clarke, 'very good' and, according to *Hugh Johnson's 2008 Pocket Wine Book* (Mitchell Beazley) 'well worth trying'. At Carr Taylor, based near Hastings, it is possible to buy sparkling wines, whilst across the county line in Kent, the Barnsole vineyard, planted in 1993, has regularly been awarded quality status and therefore it must be worth tasting a bottle or two of their wines! Down the road at Biddenden, there is a vineyard that was planted nearly forty years ago and, not only does it produce wine, but also, as you might expect in Kent, good cider and apple juice. In Kent, it is also possible to buy wines from the Chapel Down, Tenterton and Lamberhurst vineyards – all part of the English Wines Group. Essex producers of note include Carters, Mersea and New Hall.

CAMBRIDGESHIRE, SUFFOLK, OXFORDSHIRE, LEICESTERSHIRE AND HERTFORDSHIRE

In Cambridgeshire, Chilford Hall's 'Aulric de Norsehide' is a past trophy winner, whilst at Gifford's Hall near Bury-St-Edmunds, in Suffolk, it is possible to find wines that have been oak-aged. Also based near Bury-St-Edmunds is Wyken vineyard. Another Suffolk trophy winner is the Shawsgate vineyard at Framlingham. Boze Down in Oxfordshire, has a wide range of high quality wines and, unusually for most English vineyards, some interesting reds. At Chiltern Valley, near Henley, the grapes from its tiny vineyard are augmented by those from other growers in order to produce Old Luxters Dry Reserve. The Madeleine Sylvaner wins medals for its producers at Eglantine near Loughborough and, at Frithsden, Hertfordshire, the Ortega and Kerner are worth trying.

GLOUCESTERSHIRE, WORCESTERSHIRE, SHROPSHIRE, HEREFORDSHIRE AND WALES

Three Choirs Vineyards, based in Gloucestershire, grow the Bacchus and Huxelrebe grapes and produce 'English Nouveau', which is generally very good and very popular. Three Choirs also take grapes from other vineyards and produce wines on their behalf.

One such is at Broadfield Court where, in 1971, Keith James began his vineyard with a modest planting of some fifty vines in the walled garden. The original grape varieties of Mueller Thurgau and Seyve Villard have now been joined by Reichensteiner, Huxelrebe, Madeleine Angevine and lately, the red Pinot Noir. From these varieties, the six wines on the Bodenham English wines list are produced singly and in blends and are available to taste and purchase in Broadfield's own shop and café. Interestingly, bearing in mind what was said about certain foods complementing wines better than others, the café specializes in producing a menu that works well with their wines.

Vineyards in Worcestershire include Astley and Tiltridge. Near Shrewsbury, a Roman settlement has been used as a vineyard for several years now and, unsurprisingly, the origins of the site have influenced the name Wroxeter Roman. Beeches vineyard at Ross-on-Wye produces a dry white and at Coddington can be found a good Bacchus grape.

Glyndwr vineyard, near Llanblethain is the oldest commercial vineyard in Wales and Llanerch, South Glamorgan, produce wines sold under the 'Cariad' label. At Worthenbury, the grapes of Pinot Noir, Chardonnay and Sauvignon Blanc are produced with the aid of poly-tunnels, whilst Sugar Loaf is the origin of some fantastic award-winning wines.

To Make a Classic Sloe Gin

Pick the sloes in the autumn, but don't worry about the traditionalists who insist that the fruit should not be picked until it has had a frost on it – it makes no difference at all to the end product. Again according to the traditionalists, each sloe must be pricked with a fork, but that is very time-consuming and tedious and we find that it is easiest to bruise them and split the skin by using the end of a wooden rolling pin. Alternatively, freeze them for a few days, after which time the skins will have burst.

450g/1lb sloes
225g/8oz caster or brown sugar
1 bottle gin (use the strongest proof you can find)

Place the prepared sloes into a wide-necked screw-top glass container, add the sugar and the gin and screw the lid on tightly. Shake daily for a few days, every other day for a few more and then once a week for a couple of months. Sloe gin made in early October should be ready to drink by Christmas, but the longer you keep it, the better it will be. Make Blackberry Brandy using the same method, except that it is obviously not necessary to prick the fruit.

COUNTRY WINES AND LIQUEURS

Long before wines were made from grapes, the early Britons were drinking fruit wines and mead made from honey. Traditionally hidden at the back of the cupboard, country wines and liqueurs are normally treated with alarm and suspicion! Try serving Granny's traditional recipes *with* food rather than as either an aperitif or, worse still, after a meal that has already been accompanied by a serious amount of alcohol. A gooseberry wine, for example, goes well with smoked fish, an elderberry with meat dishes (and some cheeses) whilst plum is good with duck, venison and other game such as pheasant and grouse.

Country wine is made from the flowers, berries, leaves and roots of plants that grow wild. The purest and most perfect of them are easily made and with the simplest and cheapest of equipment. To make elderflower wine for example, you would need only florets (how many depends on the strength of flavour you like in your wine, boiling water, dried yeast, a quantity of sugar and assorted fermentation jars, bottles, a funnel, some tubing with which to siphon off the wine, a plastic bucket with a lid and the patience to wait a year whilst it matures.

The only limit to making a good liqueur from what is available in the countryside is your imagination. Almost anything can be used, but the most popular are those made from sloes (fruits of the blackthorn), wild damsons and cherries, and blackberries. The spirit is usually gin or brandy, although vodka and those lethal spirits that you brought back from holiday and now sit lurking at the very back of the drinks cabinet can also be used to good effect!

The simplest method is to place fruit, sugar and alcohol into a Kilner jar or similar container with an airtight lid. Place it on a windowsill and shake it daily for about a month before straining, bottling and storing in a cool place for a few months more. Extra flavours can be gained by using honey instead of sugar or adding herbs such as marjoram and spices such as nutmeg, ginger or cinnamon. Use 'chunks' or grated spices, rather than ground, as it's impossible to strain out the powder, which will impart an unpleasant sawdust taste and feel when it is drunk.

ATHOLL BROSE

Although the Scottish climate cannot hope to sustain a serious wine-making culture, there is, apparently, a form of liquid psychological warfare that has been used against rival clans for many generations. Basically, all that is required is to get them drunk with Atholl Brose and they will be incapable of anything! It is a technique which has reputedly worked very well for the Atholl family in Perthshire – so well in fact that their name has now become attached to the mixture, which uses oatmeal, whisky and heather honey. Before law suits start flying, let it be said that there is no real substance to the allegation, but the legend of the family's brose exploits emerges first in the fifteenth century when an Atholl earl is reputed to have used the mixture to rid the Scottish king of a particularly troublesome Lord of the Isles. Another story has it that a young man in the area managed to rid the district of a wild savage by employing the intoxicating liquor and then claimed as his reward the hand in marriage of a young Atholl heiress. Make some if you dare!

1 bottle Scotch whisky
300ml/10fl oz double cream
450g/1lb honey
whites of 6 eggs
1 handful oatmeal

Soak the oatmeal in Scotch whisky. Beat the egg whites until stiff, then fold cream into them. Add the honey. Very slowly blend in the whisky and oatmeal. Pour into bottles and store for a week, shaking (the bottles, not yourself!) occasionally.

COMMERCIALLY PRODUCED WINES AND LIQUEURS

There are, throughout the country, many producers of traditional country wines and liqueurs. Located between Petworth and Midhurst in West Sussex, the Lurgashall Winery produces 500,000 bottles of country wines, meads and liqueurs every year – a trip to Google or similar internet search engine will locate others. At one end of the British Isles is the Porthallow Vineyard situated on the Lizard Peninsula of Cornwall, whilst in Scotland, the George Strachan Ltd website is able to supply you with fermentations and distillations from the Shetland Isles, the Hebrides, the mainland Highlands and the Lowlands.

TIPS FOR STORAGE

Traditionally, bottles of wine are always stored on their sides to ensure that the corks do not dry out, and even screw-tops are best stored this way in order to allow for settlement of any sediment. Always choose a dark area as your wine 'cellar' and keep them well away from anything that may cause the wine to become tainted as a result of an unwanted taste being introduced through the porous cork – the garden shed might be good in that it is cool, dark and undisturbed, but it would be a shame if your wine tastes of over-wintered garlic or lawn-mower petrol as a result of sharing the same space! If you have to keep your wine in a light place, cover with a heavy blanket, wrap individual bottles in paper or, by far the simplest solution, keep them in the boxes in which they were bought.

Many kitchen designers nowadays include wine racks as part of their fixtures and fittings; the kitchen is, however, not necessarily the best place to keep wine because it could be too warm and light. If you must store your bottles in the kitchen, remember that warm air rises, so put bottles of red wine at the top of your rack and the whites at the bottom where it is cooler. The ideal temperature for storing (not serving – which is a totally different ball-game altogether) wine is anywhere between 6–14°C (43–57°F) and, if you want to get technical, should have a humidity rating of between 55–75 per cent – so keep well away from your central heating boiler! Also avoid storing in the utility room next to the washing machine or tumble dryer because the resultant vibrations will be continually stirring up any sediment. In an ordinary house devoid of cellars and *sommeliers*, the cupboard under the stairs is probably your best bet.

Wine, cheese and grapes – a classic combination?

Glossary

Al dente – An Italian term, usually referring to pasta, used to describe the texture of slight resistance when bitten.

Appellation – A designated wine-growing area, as defined under local laws.

Arborio rice – Short, fat, starchy rice. Usually used to make risotto.

Arrowroot – Sometimes used as a substitute for cornflour as a thickening agent; unlike cornflour, it produces a clear sauce.

Au gratin – A method of finishing a cooked dish by covering it with sauce or breadcrumbs or both.

Bain-marie – A shallow-sided container, which is half-filled with water kept just below boiling point and in which containers of food are placed to keep warm or cook without over-heating. A bain-marie is used for cooking custards and a roasting tin is suitable for the purpose.

Bard – To cover lean meat, game or poultry with strips of pork fat or bacon to prevent it from drying out during cooking.

Basmati rice – A long-grain, nutty flavoured rice.

Baste – To brush food as it cooks with butter, meat drippings, or stock in order to keep baked or roasted foods moist.

Béchamel sauce – A French white sauce made with milk and a roux of butter and flour.

Beurre blanc – French sauce made with wine, vinegar and shallots reduced over heat, into which butter is whisked until the sauce is thick.

Beurre manié – A sauce thickener of softened butter combined with an equal amount of flour.

Bisque – A thick seafood soup.

Blanch – A cooking technique of placing food into boiling water for a short time, then in cold water to stop cooking.

Bouillabaisse – A French seafood stew.

Bouillon – A strained broth made by cooking, vegetables, meat, seafood, or poultry in water and used in soups and sauces.

Bouquet garni – Herbs tied or bagged in muslin and used to flavour soups or casseroles.

Braise – To cook slowly in a small amount of liquid in a covered pot. Meats are usually browned prior to braising in order to seal them. Braising can be done on top of the stove or in an oven, depending on the recipe.

Brining – Immersing food in a strong salt and water solution.

Butterfly – A preparation technique of splitting poultry down the centre, nearly completely through, so the halves can be opened and cooked flat.

B vitamins – Water-soluble vitamins that make up what is known as the B-complex. They can be known by either numbers or names, or sometimes both.

Caramelize – A cooking technique of topping a dish with sugar and then melting the sugar with high heat. Alternatively, adding sugar to a sauce as it is being made in a pan.

Carbohydrates – A collective term for starches and fibre.

Carbonade – A rich stew of braise of meat including beer.

Caul – A fatty membrane taken from pig or sheep, used to wrap preparations, such as pâté, which melts on cooking.

Celeriac – The root of a variety of celery, used raw or cooked in a variety of dishes.

Chafing dish – A dish kept above a heat source to keep food warm.

Chervil – A mild, aniseed-flavoured herb related to parsley.

Chiffonade – Thin strips of vegetables lightly sautéed or used raw to garnish soups.

Chining – Severing the rib-bones from the backbone by sawing through the ribs near to the spine to make chops or cutlets.

Chorizo – A highly seasoned, coarsely ground pork sausage flavoured with chillies, garlic and spices.

Clarified butter – Butter with milk solids removed. Easy to make by melting butter in a bowl until the solids settle to the bottom (chill until hardened, turn over, and skim off the solids).

Cocotte – Small earthenware, ovenproof pot of single portion size (also known as 'Ramekin').

Confit – Usually meat, particularly duck (and goose), preserved in fat, but can on occasions include fish (see 'Confit of Salmon' page 27).

Creaming – To beat an ingredient or ingredients with a spoon or beaters until light and fluffy.

Crown roast – A preparation of meat, where a rib section is tied in a circle with the rib-ends up.

Cut-in – To work a solid fat, such as butter, shortening or lard, into dry ingredients.

Dariole – Individual cup-shaped mould used for making puddings, jellies and creams.

De-bone – To remove the bones from meat or poultry – best done with a flexible knife so that it is possible to get as close to the bone as possible without losing meat.

Deglaze – The addition of liquid (usually stock or wine) to a pan of cooked meat, followed by stirring to loosen the stuck bits of meat from the pan.

Devein – To remove the vein from the back of a shrimp.

Devil – To mix with spicy or hot seasonings.

Dice – To cut food into small cubes of about 5mm (¼in) across.

Egg wash – To apply a mixture of beaten egg (or egg/milk mix) over pastry in order to give an attractive glaze.

Emulsify – See 'Emulsion'.

Emulsion – A mixture of two liquids that do not normally mix well and achieved by rapid stirring and slowly pouring one liquid into another.

En croûte – A term describing food that is wrapped in pastry prior to cooking.

En papillote – French for 'in a paper casing' and refers to food cooked in a parchment or foil-wrapped.

Escalope – Thin slice of meat, often fried in breadcrumbs.

Faggot – Most commonly, a small ball made from pork offal, onion and breadcrumbs, but also an alternative regional name for a bouquet garni.

Falafel – A mixture of beans, peas, ground cumin, salt and pepper, and coriander.

Farcé – French name for stuffing.

Fines herbes – A mixture of finely chopped herbs, traditionally chervil, chives, parsley and tarragon.

Flake – To separate fish gently into small pieces – usually with a fork.

Flambé – Where alcohol is added to food, warmed and then ignited.

Fold – To gently mix two or more ingredients together, where one is usually heavier than the other, in order to combine but preserve the texture of each.

Fricassée – White stew of chicken, rabbit, veal, or vegetables, finished with cream and egg yolks and often served with rice.

Galantine – A mixture of cooked meats or poultry set in their own jelly and served cold.

Garnish – To enhance finished foods with flavour or visual appeal by using other edible products such as herbs, fruit slices, small vegetables or even edible flowers.

Giblets – Edible internal organs of poultry and game, including the liver, heart and gizzard.

Glaze – The process of dipping or brushing to give flavour and a shiny finish to roasted meats and pastries.

Gremolata – Very finely chopped lemon zest, juice and parsley.

Griddle – Heavy, flat, metal plate used on top of the cooker for baking oatcakes and the like.

Hulling – Removing the stalk and leaves from soft fruits such as strawberries.

Infuse – To brew in hot water or other liquids to extract flavour.

Julienne – Sliced vegetables cut into matchstick-sized pieces, either by the use of a knife or mandolin.

Junket – English pudding made with sweetened and flavoured milk, which is then set with rennet.

Knead – To work dough with the heel of the hands in order to develop the gluten in the flour.

Kneaded butter – Softened butter mixed with flour and used to thicken soups, stocks or sauces.

Knock back – Kneading a bread mix once it has risen for the first time.

Larding – Threading small strips of fat into the surface of lean meat to prevent it from drying out during roasting.

Legumes – Any member of the pea family, including chick peas, runner beans, soya beans and lentils.

Lights – Colloquial name for the lungs of an animal, sold as offal.

Macerate – Adding liquid to food, or an ingredient, such as sugar, that causes liquid to form, in order to soften and enhance flavour after it sets for a given amount of time.

Mandolin – Not in this instance a musical instrument, but a slicer used to produce Julienne vegetables.

Marinade – A liquid and/or herb mix in which meat and game is left for several hours. *See also* 'Marinate'.

Marinate – To add liquid or dry ingredients (or a mixture of the two, such as wine and herbs) to meat or fish in order to impart flavour or tenderize.

Meuniére – Applies to food cooked in butter, seasoned with salt, pepper and lemon juice and finished with parsley. Most commonly associated with fish dishes.

Mille feuilles – A type of pastry made with thin crispy puff pastry.

Mixed spice – Classically, a mixture containing caraway, all-spice, coriander, cumin, nutmeg and ginger.

Omega-3 – Desirable essential fatty acid found in oily fish (and also rapeseed oil and walnuts).

Oxidation – Chemical process in which a substance combines with oxygen; for example, when an apple turns brown after it has been peeled or cut open.

Pan-fry – To brown and cook foods in fat in a shallow pan, where the fat does not completely cover the food.

Parboil – To partially cook food by boiling briefly in water.

Parfait – Frozen dessert made with cream and puréed fruit.

Patty tin – Moulded baking tin, usually used for making small cakes.

Pectin – Substance found in fruit, and is required for setting jams.

Pinch – An approximate measure of any ingredient, but usually an amount held between thumb and forefinger.

Poaching – Cooking food in gently simmering (not boiling) liquid.

Proving – Term used to describe bread dough left to rise after shaping.

Purée – To process foods into a smooth substance, usually by the aid of a blender, processor, or pestle and mortar.

Raita – A mix of natural yoghurt and cucumber.

Ramekin – *See* 'Cocotte'.

Reduce – To boil a liquid rapidly until it partially evaporates, leaving a thicker texture and more intense flavour.

Refresh – Most commonly used in reference to blanched vegetables that are placed immediately in ice water to stop the cooking, set the colour and restore the crispness. Greens and herbs that are still very fresh, but have gone limp, can be restored to their original state by placing in cold water and then patted dry.

Rennet – A substance used for making Junket and other puddings.

Roulade – French name given to foods wrapped into a roll: for example, cream cheese spread onto a slice of cold roast ham, which is then rolled and prepared as a simple starter.

Roux – A cooked mixture of flour and butter used as a thickener of sauce or soup.

Sachet – A small pouch, similar to a tea-bag, filled with dried herbs.

Sauté – To fry foods quickly in a little fat such as olive oil or butter, until tender and lightly browned.

Saturated fat – The predominant type of fat in meat and dairy products – too great an intake has been proven to cause a higher risk of heart disease.

Scald – Plunging foods with skins, such as tomatoes, into boiling water to loosen and split the skin in order to remove it easily.

Scoring – Cutting narrow parallel lines in the surface of food either to improve its appearance or help it cook more quickly and evenly.

Seal – To cook meats quickly on all sides over high heat to brown and seal in the juices (also known as 'Sear').

Seasoned flour – Flour with salt and pepper added, and used to dust meat or fish before frying or stewing.

Skimming – To remove and discard froth or fat from the surface of stock or stews.

Souse – To cover food – usually fish – with a mixture of vinegar, spices and water, in which mixture the fish is afterwards cooked.

Stabilizers – Substances that help to stabilize the structure of food and help prevent any unwanted chemical changes as well as to help it thicken. Gelatin and pectin are examples of commonly used stabilizers.

Stock – A strained broth made from cooking vegetables, meat, or seafood in water which is then used as a base for soups and sauces.

Sweat – Cooking foods, such as onions, over medium heat until they soften without burning and browning.

Tabbouleh – A mixture of bulgur wheat, parsley, mint, spring onions, cucumber and tomato.

Tenderizing – Beating raw meat with a wooden mallet, rolling pin, or heel of the hand.

Tournedos – Beefsteak cut from tenderloin.

Translucent – Cooking until clear or transparent.

Truss – Technique of stitching or wrapping poultry with string to keep it compact and secure when cooking.

Veloute – A type of sauce.

Verjus – Sour juice from unripe grapes and added to sauces in order to increase flavour.

Vinaigrette – A basic oil and vinegar combination used over salads (and sometimes, cold vegetables or cold meat dishes).

Welsh onions – Perennial and excellent substitute for spring onions. Use the leaves in place of chives.

Yellow stainer – Common name for the poisonous *Agaricus xanthodermus* mushroom, which grows in the same conditions as the edible field mushroom. BE CERTAIN OF THE IDENTIFICATION OF ANY FUNGI BEFORE COOKING.

Zest – The coloured rind of citrus fruit, normally grated or cut into thin slivers and used as additional flavouring. Zest contains vital oils, but to avoid a bitterness of taste, grate or pare the rind thinly, avoiding the pith.

Index

Actual recipes are shown in italics